Judaism
on Illness
and Suffering

Judaism
on Illness
and Suffering

REUVEN P. BULKA

JASON ARONSON INC.
Northvale, New Jersey
Jerusalem

This book was set in 12 pt. Antiqua by Alpha Graphics of Pittsfield, New Hampshire.

10 9 8 7 6 5 4 3 2 1

Library of Congress Cataloging-in-Publication Data

Bulka, Reuven P.
  Judaism on illness and suffering / by Reuven P. Bulka.
    p.   cm.
  Includes bibliographical references and index.
  ISBN 0-7657-5986-1
    1. Medicine—Religious aspects—Judaism.   2. Pain—Religious
aspects—Judaism.   3. Suffering—Religious aspects—Judaism.
  I. Title.
  BM538.H43B85   1997
  296.3'118—dc21   97-9660

Manufactured in the United States of America. Jason Aronson Inc. offers books and cassettes. For information and catalog write to Jason Aronson Inc., 230 Livingston Street, Northvale, NJ 07647.

In Memory of
my dear Mehutan

Rabbi Yaakov Yosef Shonek
27 Nisan, 5699—13 Nisan, 5757

A man of
unbending faith,
indomitable courage,
unyielding commitment,
and total dedication
to family, community, and posterity

Contents

Acknowledgments

A number of people have made important contributions to this book in its final form.

The original impetus for this book came from my son-in-law's mother, Mrs. Arlene Shonek. From her we have gained insight into the meaning of dedication. From her husband, my *mehutan*, Rabbi Yaakov Shonek, we have learned the extent to which faith can overcome adversity.

I am grateful to the helmsman at Jason Aronson, Arthur Kurzweil, for pushing me firmly but gently to finish the manuscript. As always, he and his helpful staff put out a superior product with warmth and efficiency. Thanks to Steve Palmé of Jason Aronson Inc. for a superb editing job. Rabbi Walter Wurzburger, distinguished scholar and dear friend, read the original manuscript with great care, and offered invaluable suggestions that have greatly improved the final version.

My wife and editor once again gave the manuscript the benefit of her stylistic scalpel. It reads much better, thanks to her.

Blanche Osterer was, as always, helpful with typing certain parts of this manuscript.

Roslyn Frankl graciously volunteered to read the manuscript, and her editorial scrutiny was most useful in enhancing the text.

Primarily, I am grateful to the many people I have been privileged to know who, in their unique ways, have been true inspirations. Many are no longer alive, but their surpassing courage and unrelenting faith remain vibrant and invigorating standards to which we can and should aspire.

Introduction

Writing a book about illness and suffering from a Jewish perspective is a daunting task. Certainly, attempting to determine a rationale for illness that covers all contingencies is an exercise in arrogance and is, at the same time, doomed to failure.

To understand all illness and the ultimate purpose behind illness is to enter the domain of God. Human beings dare not step into the celestial sphere. One need only contemplate the sheer incomprehensibility of Tay-Sachs disease, Canavan's, Functional Dysautonomia, or other illnesses afflicting children to realize how far we are from making sense of life and its illnesses.

The purpose of this book is not to invade God's province; nor is it to offer a comprehensive, exhaustive study of the Jewish view on illness and suffering. The purpose is merely to expand our own horizons; to place a perspective on illness and suffering that will better enable us to live, to cope, and to endure within the confines of our finiteness.

This book does not propose to answer all questions, but it does not question the need to seek answers. We attempt to place the issues into a clear perspective, one that will enable those who are ill, and their family constellation, to better confront their challenging situations. The book is a combination of theology, philosophy, and psychology, a combination of discourse and anecdote, a combination of theory and practical advice. It does not pretend to cover all bases, only to touch on major themes and concerns. Some themes and sources are cited more often than others, for emphasis and to reinforce certain points.

In the midst of writing this book, Israel was rocked with a series of brutal and devastating suicide attacks—in Jerusalem, Ashkelon, and Tel Aviv. These bombs, designed to kill and maim the greatest number of people possible, left over sixty people dead and hundreds wounded.

It is impossible for those of us living in the relative comfort and quiet of societies less vulnerable to such acts of terrorism to truly understand the depth of the personal and collective grief of the affected families. Nevertheless, I asked myself a simple question: Would this book help any of these families in their time of anguish? I could not, in good conscience, return a confident "yes"; the best I could do was a "definite maybe."

This left me wondering whether, in the light of this truth, it was worthwhile to finish this book and to publish it. After grappling with this, I finally asked myself a sobering question: Does any book exist that would definitely be a comfort and a help to all these families? If such a book were possible, it would have been written long ago.

The fact is that different books help different people. None help all, and all help some. I fervently hope that this book will help some people as they wrestle with illness; help them toward spiritual recovery as they do their best to attain physical recovery.

I must bring one caution to the reader's attention at the outset. I will not try to reinvent Jewish tradition or to present a slant on the subject of illness and suffering that is more pleasing to the ear but that is not authentic Judaism. It would be irresponsible for anyone wrestling with this vital issue to distort what Judaism says just because it sounds better or is closer to what we think Judaism ought to say.

To present the Judaic view on this or any other matter demands that one do so honestly, even if what is presented may at times seem harsh and insensitive. Such is the case with this book. The presentation may at times seem severe, but I urge the reader to stick with it. There is gentle light, and much of it, at the end of this harsh tunnel.

I

PAIN AND ENJOYMENT

1

Enjoying the World

Illness and suffering are virtually unavoidable over the course of a complete life. This fact of life is eloquently explained by Maimonides, in his volume *The Guide of the Perplexed.*

The first species of evil is that which befalls man because of the nature of coming-to-be and passing-away, I mean to say because of his being endowed with matter. Because of this, infirmities and paralytic afflictions befall some individuals either in consequence of their original natural disposition, or they supervene because of changes occurring in the elements, such as corruption of the air or a fire from heaven and a landslide. We have already explained that divine wisdom has made it obligatory that there should be no coming-to-be except through passing-away. Were it not for the passing-away of the individuals, the coming-to-be relating to the species would not

continue. Thus that pure beneficence, that mu-
nificence, that activity causing good to overflow,
are made clear. He who wishes to be endowed
with flesh and bones and at the same time not
be subject to impressions [change] and not to be
attained by any of the concomitants of matter
merely wishes, without being aware of it, to combine two contraries, namely, to be subject to impressions and not to be subject to them. For if he
were not liable to receive impressions, he would
not have been generated, and what exists of him
would have been one single individual and not
a multitude of individuals belonging to one species (Moses Maimonides, *The Guide of the Perplexed*, trans. by Shlomo Pines, Chicago: University of Chicago Press, 1963, 3:12, pp. 443–444).

It is one thing for illness to be unavoidable; it
is another to actually seek out illness and suffering.
The fundamental imperative to affirm life that is
incumbent upon us means that we should enjoy
and appreciate all the good that God has placed in
the world for us.

Consider the well-known story told of Rabbi
Samson Rafael Hirsch, a great rabbinic luminary of
the past generation, who, in his later years, one day
asked his students to take him to the Alps. The students were happy to oblige their great teacher, but
they did wonder about the reason for their Rav's
request. He explained to them that he knew the
time for going to meet his Maker was approaching,
and that he would be asked many questions. He
contemplated the possibility, even the likelihood,

that God would ask him: "Nu, Shimshon, did you see my lovely Alps?" Rabbi Hirsch did not want to disappoint God by having to answer "no."

Why did Rabbi Hirsch think that God would ask a question like this? Because the wondrous sights of the world are part of the beauty of the world, and the beauty of the world is there for us to experience; it is one of the ways through which we appreciate God's greatness. We dare not deny ourselves the opportunity for such fulfillment. We will have to answer for refraining from fully appreciating God's world (Jerusalem Talmud, *Kiddushin* 4:12).

It would be misleading to suggest that denial has no place in Jewish tradition. The Talmud records a debate concerning whether one who fasts is considered a sinner or a holy person (*Taanit*, 11a–b). The halakhic consensus is that if one is healthy enough to make it through the fast, then that person is considered holy for having fasted. However, if one cannot endure such fasting, then proceeding with the fast brands that person as a sinner (*Shulhan Arukh*, Orah Hayyim 571:1).

Nevertheless, for one who desires to fast, it is considered preferable that this take the form of refraining not from eating, but from talking. This will cause no damage or weakness to the body, and is likely to produce the same spiritual benefits (*Mishnah Berurah*, Orah Hayyim 571, note 2).

Regarding the actual experiencing of pleasure, we need to draw a fine but distinctive line between engaging in pleasure just for pleasure's sake, and

engaging in pleasure for meaning's sake. Nevertheless, pleasure is a vital component of life, and basic
to apprehending God's majesty.

Meaningful pleasure is to be pursued; pain is
to be avoided. This is not only a fundamental, theoretical principle of Judaism; it is at the same time a
principle that is reinforced with a significant number of rules and regulations regarding pleasure and
pain.

On the positive side, we are obliged to "Rejoice
in all of the good that God has given to you"
(Deuteronomy 26:11). We are asked to maintain a
positive focus, to "Serve God in joy" (Psalms 2:11).
Masochists may be happy when in pain, but normal people are saddened by pain. If we are urged
to be meaningfully happy, this suggests a life relatively unencumbered by pain. Despite the sadness
associated with pain, it is possible, even desirable,
to maintain this cheerful, positive focus even in illness and suffering, a matter that is discussed later.

In general, there are no direct *mitzvots* (obligations) within Judaism that oblige us to experience pain. It may well be that there are times
when the actualization of a command or the adherence to a prohibition may involve pain, but the
experience of the pain is never the direct focus of
the command.

The fact that there are no commandments to
experience pain is a definitive statement that the
experience of pain, in itself, is not a commandment,
and is more likely than not a detraction from life
and from the affirmation of God. That some commandments may tangentially involve pain is an

accident that is not necessarily unavoidable. In certain circumstances and for certain individuals, commandments may bring the experience of pain, but that is not the intent of the observance, nor is it a necessary quality of the observance.

On occasion, the fact that there may be pain in the fulfillment of a commandment renders the person so pained exempt from the fulfillment of it. The well-known statement that one who is in pain is exempt from sitting in the *sukkah* (tabernacle) on the festival of Sukkot is an example of this. One who cannot tolerate the cold of the *sukkah* need not sit in the *sukkah*; nor is anyone obliged, or even encouraged, to sit there when significant rain is pouring through (*Shulhan Arukh*, Orah Hayyim 640:4; 639:5–7).

This exemption is linked to the notion that the *sukkah* is one's abode during the festival, and anything that would cause one to leave the house renders one exempt from living in the *sukkah*. Additionally, the pain exemption is linked to the obligation to rejoice in the festival (see *Shulhan Arukh*, Orah Hayyim 529). Such rejoicing is compromised if one is in pain.

A few commandments do seem to be associated with pain. One example is the obligation to fast on the Day of Atonement (Leviticus 23:26–32). Tradition ascribes to Yom Kippur a sense of forgiveness and joy, historically linked to the atonement extended to the Israelites after the Golden Calf episode—atonement that manifested itself in the transmission of a new set of tablets that were handed down on Yom Kippur, the Day of Atonement (*Taanit* 30b). Yom Kippur was actually a day of great celebration in the Jewish calendar (*Taanit* 26b).

Yet Yom Kippur, the Day of Atonement, is a day of total abstinence. From before sundown just prior to the Day of Atonement until nighttime at the close of the Day of Atonement—a period usually lasting close to twenty-six hours—no eating, drinking, washing, anointing of the skin, or wearing of leather shoes is permitted (*Shulhan Arukh*, Orah Hayyim 612, 613, 614). In addition, marital relations are also proscribed (ibid., 615). On the Day of Atonement, which is referred to in the Bible as a Shabbat (Leviticus 23:32), all the work restrictions in force on *Shabbat* are likewise in effect (*Shulhan Arukh*, Orah Hayyim 611:2).

Fasting can be a painful experience, and yet the fulfillment of the letter and the spirit of Yom Kippur, the Day of Atonement, is totally divorced from the notion of pain.

Those who assume that, by subjecting themselves to pain and sacrifice for an entire day, they are thereby fulfilling the wishes of God, are making a serious mistake (see Isaiah 58:5). On the other hand, those who think that they have compromised the meaning of Yom Kippur because they made it through the day without feeling hungry are also mistaken.

Yom Kippur is a day of total, uncompromising meditation. It is a day when the human being is divorced from material concerns of all sorts, even eating and drinking. It is a day when one is forced, by virtue of the hedge of legislation surrounding the day, to focus inward; to examine the nature of one's deeds over the past year; to repent of all wrong that has been committed; and to express regret over all worthy acts that could have been carried out, but were not (see Maimonides, *Mishnah Torah*, *Laws of Repentance* 2:1–2; 6–7).

Yom Kippur also involves resolve for the future—to correct the wrongs of the past; to redress situations that call for compensation; and to embark on a qualitatively superior life as a result of the atonement experience (ibid. 2:4).

The biblical prescription for Yom Kippur indicates that such total meditation cannot be achieved when one is involved in the material world; therefore, a total detachment from the material world is prescribed. It is likely that individuals who wholeheartedly embrace this meditative spirit will be oblivious to their own physical condition, and may not even be aware of the hunger and the thirst that normally plague those deprived of sustenance for so long. When one transcends the self into the dimension of meditation, physical concerns may effectively retreat into the background.

On the other hand, individuals who observe Yom Kippur by clock-watching to see how much longer they must endure the agony of fasting, but who achieve nothing in the realm of serious meditation and resolution, may be experiencing real pain, but they are not truly experiencing the Day of Atonement.

The observance of Yom Kippur is the command that comes closest to legislating the experience of pain. Yet, upon analysis, Yom Kippur, though it may tangentially involve pain, is certainly neither philosophically nor causally linked directly to the experience of pain.

Another commandment ostensibly associated with pain is the obligation to circumcise newborn boys (Leviticus 12:3). Circumcision, although it involves only the removal of a foreskin, is undoubtedly painful. Nevertheless, the pain is not the essential component of the procedure. Witness the fact that a boy who is born without a foreskin—literally born circumcised—need not go through a painful procedure in order to effect the covenantal pact. A relatively simple and painless procedure is prescribed for such a contingency (*Shulhan Arukh*, Yoreh De'ah 263:4).

Also, the circumcision procedure takes place when the child is only eight days old (Leviticus 12:3). Since circumcision signifies entry into the covenant, it would be logical for this covenantal act to take place when the child reaches maturity—at bar mitzvah—and understands the meaning of what is transpiring. It may be conjectured that circumcision performed at such an early age is much less painful than that performed later on, when the boy's nerve endings are more developed. To avoid pain, the Torah assigns circumcision to the eighth day.

Another instance of a pain-related obligation is the first commandment of the Torah, "Be fruitful and multiply" (Genesis 1:28; 9:7). The fulfillment of procreation starts off with an intensely pleasurable experience, the sexual union. However, roughly nine months later, the woman experiences excruciating pain—the pain of childbirth, a pain so intense that it is referred to in the Torah as *etzev*, signifying renunciation (following the translation of Rabbi Samson Raphael Hirsch, Genesis 3:16).

An interesting anomaly concerning the commandment to procreate is the fact that it is the man who is obliged to "be fruitful and multiply" (*Yevamot* 65b), and it is thus the man who fulfills the commandment when a child is born (*Shulhan Arukh*, Even Ha'Ezer 1:5). The woman is not commanded to be fruitful and multiply; when she gives birth, she does not fulfill the commandment, since she is not obligated to do so.

It seems unfair that the woman, who carries the child within her for nine months, with all the attendant risks and discomforts of pregnancy, should not even be given the *credit* for having persevered through such trying circumstances.

However, giving birth is painful—during labor, during the birth itself, and even for a significant period after birth. Were the woman obligated to have children, it would be an instance of legislated pain. It would be a biblically ordained imperative to undergo pain—unavoidable pain, in most instances—for the purpose of fulfilling a commandment.

The Torah directs the obligation to have children to the man, who is not involved in the process beyond conception, does not go through intense labor, and does not endure the pain associated with childbirth. The woman has no obligation to have children, because she cannot be obligated to suffer pain. She may desire children despite the pain of the labor and the birth process, but that is primarily her decision rather than a biblically imposed duty (see detailed discussion of this entire issue in Reuven P. Bulka, *Judaism on Pleasure* [Northvale, New Jersey: Jason Aronson, 1995], pp. 37–57).

Pain, it may be safely asserted, is not on the *mitzvah* agenda. Joy and happiness are on the agenda, but not pain.

2

Avoiding Pain

The importance of pain avoidance is evident in many diverse areas of Jewish affirmation. For example, Shmuel states that whoever "sits" in fasting is considered a sinner (*Taanit* 11a). This is related to the fact that just sitting and wallowing in fasting, and seeing fasting as an end in itself, is alien to Jewish tradition; it is considered sinful. If someone uses the fast for positive purposes, this is not seen as "sitting" in the fast, but as growing from it.

Another interesting and illuminating example surrounds the observance of the *Shabbat*. Even though it is forbidden to fast on *Shabbat* (*Shulhan Arukh*, Orah Hayyim 288:1), a person who is pained by eating is allowed to desist from eating on *Shabbat*, "since it is that one's pleasure not to eat" (Orah Hayyim 288:2, 3).

Additionally, although it is proper to eat the Friday-night *Shabbat* meal with the enhanced lumi-

nousness of the *Shabbat* candles, if these candles
are the cause of discomfort, then one is exempted
from eating in such conditions (Orah Hayyim
273:7). It is evident that even though there are specific regulations for how the *Shabbat* is to be en-
joyed, if these regulations cause an individual pain,
under certain conditions an adjustment is made so
that the *Shabbat* does not impose pain.

We need no more evidence of the general attitude to pain than to contemplate the famous talmudic explication of the all-encompassing obligation to "love your neighbor as yourself" (Leviticus
19:18). The Talmud (*Sanhedrin* 43a) states that this
means, "Choose for him an easy death." This refers
to an individual who has been given a death sentence by the rabbinical court (called the Sanhedrin). This person was to be given a drug so that he
would not feel the pain when the death sentence
was actually carried out (Maimonides, *Mishnah
Torah*, Laws of Sanhedrin 13:2).

Unnecessary pain is to be avoided, even for
someone who is about to be put to death for an
obviously serious crime. It follows quite logically
that we should, perforce, also avoid unnecessary
pain for all other individuals, who should be treated
with no less care and sensitivity than the convicted
criminal.

There is no *mitzvah* to endure pain when that
pain can be avoided, even if the avoidance is
achieved by means of strong medication.

One is not permitted to do anything to hasten
a person's demise, even if it be the removal of a
pillow from behind the individual who is teeter-

ing on the brink, because such movement may actually cause death (*Shulhan Arukh*, Yoreh De'ah 339:1). On the other hand, it is permitted to remove a hindrance to the departure of the soul—such as noise near the patient's bed—since the removal is not causing death, but rather eliminating an impediment to the natural dying process. It is clear that the intent here is directly related to a situation wherein the patient is in pain, and the removal of the impediment is therefore eminently desirable and, according to Jewish law, perfectly permissible (see Rabbi Moshe Feinstein, *Igrot Moshe*, Hoshen Mishpat 2, Bnai Brak: Ohel Yosef Printers, 1985, no. 74, part 1).

Also on this theme, the Talmud (*Mo'ed Katan* 28a) speaks about different types of death. Dying suddenly is less than desirable. Dying within the space of one day also is not desirable; dying after two days of sickness, too, is considered to be a rushed death. Death after five days of illness is deemed normal. Having seven days of sickness before dying is considered a sign of love, but beyond that is a death of affliction and suffering. In other words, it is recognized that prolonged illness preys upon the individual, is fraught with great difficulties and major challenges, and is undesirable.

Interestingly, there is a view suggested that, after a person attains the age of eighty, a sudden death is regarded as desirable; it is looked upon as "dying by the kiss" (*Mo'ed Katan* 28a).

This general and far-reaching principle concerning the avoidance of pain seems to be contradicted by a well-known talmudic statement regarding suffering: "This is the way of the Torah: to eat bread with salt, to drink water by ration, to sleep upon the ground, to live a life of hardship, and to toil in the Torah. If you do this, you will be happy and it will be well with you; *you will be happy*—in this world, *and it will be well with you*—in the World-to-Come" (*Avot* 6:4).

Is the Talmud actually recommending that pain and Torah go hand-in-hand? If so, this would be directly contradictory to the previous and explicit comments indicating the very reverse.

Our explanation of this talmudic statement is along the following lines: The Torah is so vital to the human endeavor that one must be able to endure hardships and trials in order to achieve its perceived goals. A person must be able to live on bread with salt and rationed water and sleep upon the ground, thereby living a life of hardship, and still toil in the Torah.

One must be so dedicated to the Torah that it is possible for that person to negate the material and to transcend circumstance. Once one places Torah into prominence as the essence of life, all else becomes secondary; it becomes much easier to surmount unfavorable conditions. If one is able to do this, that individual will be happy. There is a spiritual happiness in this world that far surpasses momentary pleasures. Then "it will be well with you—in the World-to-Come."

This talmudic statement is not recommending that one actually seek to deprive oneself in order to study Torah; rather, it indicates that being occupied with Torah is not consistent with rampant sensual expression. In a situation wherein the individual is faced with the painful dilemma of only being able to study Torah in adverse circumstances, then the conviction that Torah is crucial to life should make living in adverse circumstances manageable. This is not intended to mandate pain, but only to put pain into the proper perspective in the larger scheme of things.

Pain is a part of life we ought, and would probably like, to live without, but unfortunately life does not work that way. When that pain does come and we cannot avoid it, escape it, or modify it, then our obligation is to understand it and to transmute it into something positive. That transmutation is made much more likely with the realization that God may intend this pain for our own good, perhaps for a good that we may one day understand or apprehend. We can effect this reality by the way we handle the pain or the illness.

II

Difficult Questions

3

Questioning God

Illness, pain, and suffering are inextricable elements of life, but the way these are doled out leads to serious questions, theological questions, that form a basic component of Jewish tradition. The prophet Jeremiah asks: "Why does the way of the wicked prosper? Why are the workers of treachery at ease?" (Jeremiah 12:1).

The prophet Habakuk was concerned with the suffering of the righteous. "You whose eyes are too pure to look upon evil, Who cannot countenance wrongdoing, why do You countenance treachery, and stand by idle while the wicked swallows up the one that is more righteous than he?" (Habakuk 1:13).

Are any of our questions, or even complaints, to God more trenchant and direct than those of King David, who unabashedly pleaded: "Rouse Yourself, why do you sleep, O Lord? Awaken, do not reject us forever. Why do You hide Your face, ignoring our affliction and distress? We lie prostrate in the dust; our body clings to the ground. Arise and help us, redeem us, as befits Your faithfulness" (Psalms 44:24–27).

All of the psalms are an affirmation of faith and trust in God, but that does not obviate the need, even the right, to ask questions. In the end, even with the questions, "Though God slay me yet will I trust in God; but I will argue my case before God" (Job 13:15).

We can argue with God; we can question God. But this dialectic can have credibility only if it emanates from faith in God, not if it is used as an excuse for not believing in God. If there is no belief, then there can be no questions. If there is belief, then there must be questions. But are there answers?

The attempt to find answers, to grapple with the omnipotence of God in the face of evil—what is referred to as theodicy—is an age-old quest. In this quest, some components of the issue have been clarified, but the larger, overall issue remains a mystery, as much a mystery as the meaning of life itself. One cannot escape the strong feeling that this is the way it must be; that it is intended that we remain in the dark about crucial issues of life; that we not know why God has inflicted suffering. We proceed in life not with awareness of the reason for the suffering, but with faith that there is a reason.

Nahmanides, in *Sha'ar Ha'Gmul*, writes:

Our quest [concerning theodicy] is a specific one, about [the plight of] this particular man . . . . This problem is not reduced if those who fall are few in number; nor does it become more serious if their number increases. For we are not discussing [the ways of] man . . . . Our argument is instead directed towards *The Rock, His work is perfect, for all His ways are justice; there is nothing perverse or crooked in them* (Ramban [Nahmanides], *Writings & Discourses* (Vol. 2), translated and annotated by C. B. Chavel, New York: Shilo Publishing House, 1978, Gate of Reward, p. 472).*

More recently, Eliezer Berkovits wrote:

It is of course more human to query God about the suffering of the many rather than the few, but it is certainly not more humane. On the contrary, it is more ethical, and intellectually more honest and to the point, to question God about the life and happiness of which even a single soul is being cheated on this earth than to base one's doubts and quest on the sacrificial abandonment of millions (Eliezer Berkovits, *Faith After the Holocaust*, New York: Ktav Publishing House, 1973, p. 130).

Any ostensibly undeserved suffering raises questions, and certain types of undeserved punishment raise even more questions. In the words of Nahmanides:

---

*All direct quotes or translations are transmitted as rendered in the original, even though there is great discomfort with attributing gender to God. In order to be honest to the text cited, however, no changes will be made.

However, the question of a [particular] righteous man who suffers still remains. We have no propensity for seeing the world in its totality, nor [are we inclined to] investigate it in its wholeness . . . .

There are people who are born deficiently, lacking certain organs of the body. There are those who die before reaching the age of twenty years, and yet from the moment they became knowledgeable, were righteous (Ramban [Nahmanides], *Writings & Discourses* (Vol. 2), translated and annotated by C. B. Chavel, New York: Shilo Publishing House, 1978, pp. 471–472).

There is an elusive quality to the search for the rationale for suffering. Some answers address general issues to some extent, but in the end everything collapses when confronted with the question raised by Nahmanides about the suffering of children.

Generally speaking, the potential for evil is a necessary component of life. If we did not have the capacity for evil, then all our noble actions would be taken without any freedom of choice. These deeds would not be ours; they would be the actions of pre-programmed people.

However, all of Judaism is based on choosing (Deuteronomy 30:19), and choosing is possible only if there are alternatives, both good and bad. "He had to create the possibility of evil, if He was to create the possibility for its opposite, peace, goodness, love" (Berkovits, *Faith After the Holocaust*, p. 104).

As is evident from Scripture, God explicitly states that evil is God's creation (Isaiah 45:7). That same verse also attributes light and peace to God.

God has created them all, so that humans have all the options from which to choose.

If the possibility of evil exists in all of us by necessity, then we must live with the consequences of this unavoidable fact of life:

> If God did not respect man's freedom to choose his course in personal responsibility, not only would the moral good and evil be abolished from the earth, but man himself would go with them. For freedom and responsibility are of the very essence of man. Without them man is not human. If there is to be man, he must be allowed to make his choices in freedom. If he has such freedom, he will use it. Using it, he will often use it wrongly; he will decide for the wrong alternative. As he does so, there will be suffering for the innocent (Berkovits, loc. cit., p. 105).

We are thus faced with a painful choice—either no evil and no free will, and therefore no meaning to our actions; or free will and meaning, but with evil staring us in the face. Viktor Frankl, a survivor of four concentration camps, asserted that he prefers a world in which despots are possible to a world with no choices and therefore no meaning (Viktor Frankl, "The Philosophical Foundations of Logotherapy," in Erwin W. Straus, ed., *Phenomenology: Pure and Applied*, Pittsburgh: Duquesne University Press, p. 55).

Berkovits, whom we cite here somewhat extensively because he tackles the theodicy issue with intellectual vigor and Judaic rigor, carries his argument even further. In his view,

We have great understanding for the fact that
God is merciful and forgiving, that He does not
judge man harshly and is willing to have patience with him. God is waiting for the sinner to
find his way to him. This is how we like to see
God. This is how we are only too glad to acknowledge him. But we never seem to realize that while
God is long suffering, the wicked are going
about their dark business on earth and the result is ample suffering for the innocent. While
God waits for the sinner to turn to him, there is
oppression and persecution and violence among
men. Yet, there seems to be no alternative. If man
is to be, God must be long suffering with him; he
must suffer man. This is the inescapable paradox
of divine providence. While God tolerates the sinner, he must abandon the victim; while he shows
forbearance with the wicked, he must turn a deaf
ear to the anguished cries of the violated. This
is the ultimate tragedy of existence: God's very
mercy and forbearance, his very love for man,
necessitates the abandonment of some men to a
fate that they may well experience as divine in-
difference to injustice and human suffering. It is
a tragic paradox of faith that God's direct concern
for the wrongdoer should be directly responsible
for so much pain and sorrow on earth.

We conclude then: he who demands justice of
God must give up man; he who asks for God's love
and mercy beyond justice must accept suffering
(Berkovits, loc. cit., p. 106).

That God strongly desires the return of the
wicked to righteousness is evident from Scripture:
"Say unto them—As I live, says the Lord God, I have

no desire for the death of the wicked, rather that the wicked renounce the evil way and will live" (Ezekiel 33:11).

This divine forbearance has historical as well as merely personal consequences. "If man is to be, God himself must respect his freedom of decision. If man is to act on his own responsibility, without being continually over-awed by divine supremacy, God must absent himself from history. But man left to his freedom is capable of greatness in both—in creative goodness and destructive evil" (Berkovits, loc. cit., p. 107).

But what if the human capacity for evil takes over to the extent that humanity itself is destroyed? Surely, any argument for God's restraint cannot allow for total destruction. Berkovits here argues that God must be both absent and present. "That man may be, God must absent himself; that man may not perish in the tragic absurdity of his own making, God must remain present" (ibid.).

Even this stimulating and challenging discourse leaves us wanting. We can, for the moment, accept Berkovits's line of reasoning and therefore appreciate that there must be the potential for evil, and that God must be both absent to maintain human free will and present to ensure that the exercise of free will does not lead to the end of humanity. This does not preclude asking Berkovits why God could not find a less painful way of balancing matters.

Additionally, a basic question still remains: When, how, and why does God choose to intervene? We are given some indication of how God

works in a few instructive paragraphs in the Pass-
over *Haggadah*. One speaks about God keeping the
promise made to Israel.

> Blessed is [God] the keeper of God's promise to
> Israel, blessed is God. For the Holy One, blessed
> is God, took into account the end [limits of en-
> durance] to do according to that which had been
> said to our father Abraham in the covenant be-
> tween the parts, as it is written: "God said to
> Abram, 'Know with certainty that your offspring
> will be aliens in a land that is not theirs, and they
> will enslave and oppress them for four hundred
> years. And also the nation whom they shall serve
> will I judge, after which they will leave with a
> great bounty [heritage]'" (Genesis 15:13–14).

A calculated sense of timing was involved in
the redemption from Egypt. The history of Israel
up to the point of redemption is a history of suffering, but a measured suffering. God took into
account the end, the limits of endurance; how
much the people could bear before reaching the
breaking point. That is when God intervened.

The next paragraph in the *Haggadah* offers a
deeper understanding of the ultimate meaning of
God's promise to Israel, a meaning with implications in our own times.

> It is this that has sustained our ancestors and us. For
> not merely one has risen against us to annihilate us.
> Rather, in every generation they rise against us to
> annihilate us, but the Holy One, blessed is God, res-
> cues us from their hand (designs).

Implicit in the promise given by God to Abraham is the assurance that the people of Israel, no matter what they may be forced to endure, will never be destroyed. They will persevere through the worst pogroms, crusades, and mass murders. The losses may be heavy, but the people of Israel and the idea of Israel as expressed via the Torah will live on.

All this is *implicit* in the promise. In explicit terms, God spoke only about the exile and enslavement in Egypt, and the eventual redemption from bondage. Implicitly, however, the promise goes beyond the Egyptian enslavement: It is small comfort to know that your great-grandchildren will benefit from a great deliverance, but that a few generations down the road your family will be totally destroyed. The promise of deliverance applies to all of Jewish history.

It is this, the implicit nature of the promise, that has sustained our ancestors and us. We have often teetered on the brink of destruction, but at the last moment, or when hope was almost lost, God's intervention saved the day and the future.

We have assurances that even if we suffer through God's absence, that absence is not a permanent condition, and relief will always come before all hope for the future is lost. But when is that moment, and why the non-intervention till then? Only God knows.

On the personal level, even accepting that God desires the repentance of the wicked, is that repentance more important than the lives of innocent people who may be killed by the wicked on the road to repentance? This is a line of reasoning that is very difficult to justify.

Earlier we cited the view, reinforced by Berkovits, that the existence of suffering is a direct consequence of human freedom, which in itself is an absolute necessity if human life is to have any meaning. Human freedom also includes the freedom to be evil, and to be evil is to perpetrate suffering on the innocent. This is the dilemma of human existence, a dilemma that knows no explication.

We also know a type of suffering beyond that which is inflicted upon a person by other people. There is a difference between being maimed by a drunk driver and finding out that you have terminal cancer, with its concomitant agony and suffering. There is a difference between being murdered by a crazed killer and being killed by a tornado.

It is one thing to theoretically accept the existence of human evil on this earth; it is quite another to wrestle with what is obviously a divine visitation that cannot be blamed on any individual.

According to the *Zohar* (Terumah sec. 898), it seems that Jacob asked of God that a person should fall ill for two or three days and then die, in order to give the person time to instruct the household and also to repent of any sins. This request is also reported in Midrash Rabbah (Genesis 65:4). Our own life experience indicates that we have moved far beyond Jacob's request. There are people who endure protracted suffering of great intensity, and we struggle to learn the reason for this.

Consistent with one of the themes that will be developed in this book, it is important to appreciate that if God actually imposes suffering on the individual, it obviously expresses the reality that God is concerned about the individual. This is much more preferable to the notion of neglect. In the Judaic scheme of things, based on Judaic sources, God inflicts suffering upon those whom God favors.

This is done so that the individual so visited has the opportunity to correct wrongs, to effect atonement. Suffering, for this reason, is intended to spur people to realize their failings and to try to correct them. This divinely imposed suffering is not pleasant, but is ultimately for the person's benefit. This is a bitter pill to swallow, but that, too, is part and parcel of Jewish tradition, and it will be expanded upon later in this presentation.

This is a tradition that posits that God is concerned for the good people of this world, and wants them to have entrée to eternity. One of the ways this is effected is through the purging of all the individual's wrongs by means of hardships and suffering. It is those whom God likes that God afflicts. "For whom the Lord loves, the Lord rebukes, as a father the son whom he favors" (Proverbs 3:12).

It is in this sense that *Hovot Halevovot* (8:3) explains the verse, "All God's ways are merciful and truthful" (Psalms 25:10). The author explains that when something "bad" befalls a person, if it is to forgive sin, then it is *truthful*; and if what happens is part of the Godly endeavor to reward the individual for having endured this and other trials and tribulations, then it is *merciful*. In all instances, however, it is purposeful.

All this is in contradistinction to spousal or child abuse, which involves intense suffering but is devoid of meaning and purpose. Such abuse is violence, pure and simple. Abused people are more likely to visit abuse on their families, and this cruelty has no beneficial effects. Divine visitation is of an altogether different genre—different in intent, and, it is to be hoped, different in impact.

Maharal, in *Netivot Olam*, Netiv Ahavat HaShem (Love of God), Chap. 1, states that one is obliged to bless God even for the bad, since the bad is on the side of the good. This is because God does not desire bad and because we cannot endure a world wherein affliction comes upon an individual without it being an atonement for wrongdoing. Therefore, even the imposition of suffering is for the good.

This is in accord with the Midrash, which states that the phrase *v'hineh tov me'od* ("and behold, it was very good") (Genesis 1:31) is a reference to the meting out of suffering (*Genesis Rabbah* 9:10). The Midrash considers suffering to be good because it helps the person attain the eternal life of the World-to-Come.

This places a different perspective on the modern question of questions—why bad things happen to good people. At first glance this appears to be just another way of posing the age-old question: "Why do the righteous suffer?" This question is a dominant motif of modern parlance that attempts to tackle the thorny issue of suffering.

From a Judaic perspective, this question is based on a faulty premise, the premise that what is perceived to be a bad thing is, indeed, a bad thing. We experience it now as a bad thing; however, there is no Godly intent for it to be an ultimately bad thing, but only an awakening, a temporary intrusion that, in the end, will bring good.

To ask why the righteous suffer is to pose a legitimate question. To ask why bad things happen to good people may appear to be the same question couched in contemporary jargon; it is not the same question, however, because it labels suffering as bad. Suffering may not be desirable, suffering may be a reality we should endeavor to avoid, but that is a far cry from the assertion that unavoidable suffering is bad.

4

Why Do the Righteous Suffer?

Why the wicked prosper is less problematic an issue than the matter of why the righteous suffer (see Ramban [Nahmanides], *Writings & Discourses* (Vol. 2), translated and annotated by C. B. Chavel, New York, Shilo Publishing House, 1978, pp. 472–473). The prosperity of the wicked may be an act of kindness by God, but what are we to make of the suffering of the righteous? More to the point, what are those who are suffering to make of their plight?

> The conclusion of the matter [is as follows]: It is proper for any person who has suffered a mishap or some evil experience to believe that his accident and trouble are the result of his transgression and sin. He should repent for those [sins] of which he is aware, and he should confess without specification to those of which he has no recollection. If he sees *a righteous man who perisheth*

35

in his righteousness (Ecclesiastes, 7:15), he should
attribute it at first to a minimum of sins which
[that righteous man] committed. Similarly, he
should think that the peace of a wicked man
who lives at ease is due to some [act of] righteousness or good deed which he did. If his
mind subsequently urges him see [and question
the state of] a truly righteous man who is abun-
dant in merits, clean from sin, *and a pure heart*
(Proverbs, 24:4), perishing, [he should realize
that] this [enigmatic state of affairs] is not a
question [whose solution lies] within [another]
man's knowledge. [It can be resolved] only by
him who knows within himself that he is a righteous man without guilt of sin [which would ac-
count] sufficiently for the evil which has over-
taken him. He may be favorably biased toward
himself and would possibly deceive himself regarding his righteousness.

However, [concerning] this rare problem [of
the righteous who suffer] together with the more
frequent other problem of seeing an absolute
and truly wicked man succeeding in all matters
of prosperity, the perplexed person may [expect
the righteous man to be ultimately rewarded and
can] look forward to troubles which will finally
befall that wicked man (Ramban [Nahmanides],
Writings & Discourses (Vol. 2), translated and annotated by C. B. Chavel, New York: Shilo Publishing House, 1978, p. 467).

We will discuss later the matter of how the person is to comprehend the reason for the suffering.
Insofar as the theoretical side of the issue is concerned, however, Ramban relies on the argument

for the world of the ultimate. What goes on in this world is transitory; what happens later, in the ultimate world, is permanent; it is also logical as well as just in its permanence.

But for the moment—the moment being the momentary world, the world we live in, "It is not in our hands to explain either the tranquility of the wicked or even the affliction of the righteous" (*Avot* 4:18). What we do not know, and cannot know, is why some people are the exceptions to the norm. It is this that is the ultimate riddle about which the Talmud states that it is beyond our reach to explain the prosperity of the wicked and the suffering of the righteous (*Avot* 4:18), not the general belief that righteousness begets beneficial results and evil begets harmful results.

Thus, when it is asked why there are righteous people for whom things do not go well and why there are evil people for whom things go exceedingly well, the question is carefully and accurately addressed in terms of why are there exceptions. It is hard to understand the concept of a righteous person suffering, because by rights no righteous people should suffer (*Berakhot* 7a).

We cannot know the answer, and, indeed, we are probably much better off not knowing. A world that is totally logical and that fits our perceptions exactly is a world that is too patterned. It robs us of the ability to make the right decisions based on primary, intrinsic values rather than on external side benefits.

Intrinsic to the concept of embracing values for their inherent value—out of love, rather than for

side benefits—is that one should not say, "I am doing the good deed in order to receive reward in the
hereafter" (Maimonides, *Mishnah Torah*, Laws of
Repentance 10:4). But there is a significant difference between carrying out a good deed only on
condition of receiving reward, on the one hand,
and, on the other, perceiving as enduring and eternal those values that conduce toward reward in
the hereafter because they are God's formula for
life.

Whenever we are on the verge of thinking that
we have made sense out of everything, along comes
a calamity, or a totally illogical and seemingly undeserved suffering, that gives us a strong sense of
our mortality and our incapacity to grasp or explain the totality of life. But we are not God, and
we should not expect to ever attain the ability to
give logical explanations for everything. Built-in
inexplicability is part and parcel of the human dilemma, and of the human challenge.

Yes, we still question why the righteous suffer and the wicked prosper, but these questions are
asked more in terms of trying to understand what
formula is at work that would explain the entirety
of the suffering and the prosperity. Theoretically,
however, it is clear that the prosperity of the wicked
and the suffering of the righteous are not alien to
Jewish tradition; nor are they illogical in terms of
understanding the purposes behind them.

According to the Sages, the prosperity of the
wicked may be God's way of paying them for whatever good they have done by bestowing upon them
an immediate but limited reward, whereas the

suffering of the righteous is related to God's desire to purge them of any deficiency so that their ultimate reward of unencumbered eternity is not denied them (see Genesis Rabbah 33:1). Suffering then, is not an insult; neither is it necessarily a punishment. Instead, it may well be an act of kindness and concern. In the words of the *Zohar*, "Anyone who has afflictions that are brought upon that person by God, this is for atonement from sins" (*Zohar*, Aharay Mot 29).

Ultimately, however,

This question has no answer according to man's knowledge. [The explanation lies] only in the cognizance of *the God of knowledge* (1 Samuel, 2:3), blessed be He. Thus, the Rabbis related (Talmud, Menahot, 29b) concerning Rabbi Akiva that the Holy One, blessed be He, showed [Rabbi Akiva] to Moses our teacher in the vision of prophecy. [Moses] said before Him; "'Master of the Universe! You have shown me his erudition in Torah, [now] show me his reward.' Moses then saw how the Romans were cutting his flesh in a meat-market. Moses said before Him: 'Master of the Universe! This is the Torah and is this its reward?' He answered him: 'Be silent! The matter has thus entered in thought before me.'" The Sages intended to state therein that Rabbi Akiva did not deserve such a death of intolerable suffering in order to make allowance for his few evil deeds; he was thoroughly righteous all his life. [Their purport], rather, was that the matter is incomprehensible [to mortals], and it so entered the thought of the Master of thoughts, blessed be His desire and will (Ramban [Nahmanides], *Writ-*

ings & Discourses (*Vol. 2*), translated and annotated by C. B. Chavel, New York, Shilo Publishing House, 1978, pp. 453–454).

In other words, ultimately, all this is beyond
us and remains a severe test of faith. That test
of faith is more easily endured if one integrates
notions such as that suggested in the *Zohar*, to
the effect that God admonishes those that God
loves, and that God refrains from any form of rebuke for those whom God does not love (and actually, in fact, hates because of their behaviors)
(*Zohar*, B'hukkotai 42).

This means that we cannot make judgments
about the amount of suffering or enjoyment that
a person experiences in life. The suffering may or
may not be a punishment for wrongdoing; the lack
of punishment may be due to either complete righteousness or complete wickedness. It is not for us
to make judgments about others; what we do about
our own situation is another matter altogether, a
matter that commands direct and honest confrontation with ourselves.

King David says: "I will raise the cup of salvation and call the name of God" (Psalms 116:13).
But he also says that "pain and agony I will find.
But I will call in the name of God; please, God,
deliver my soul" (Psalms 116:3–4). Our relationship to God is not contingent on the good times
that we enjoy; it is, in fact, unconditional. That
unconditionality is itself made more viable by the
realization that the pain and the agony are temporary, and are intended for long-term benefit.

5

Why Do
Children Suffer?

The pain and suffering of children is a major obstacle to any coherent understanding of God's ways. The question of children's suffering must be posed, however, even in light of the enormous difficulty in understanding it.

I will go still further and say that it is even possible for a completely guiltless individual to be subjected to trials in order to be compensated for them afterwards, for I find that children are made to suffer pain, and I have no doubt about their eventual compensation for these sufferings. The sorrows brought upon them by the All-Wise, might, therefore, be compared to the discipline that their father might administer to them in the form of flogging or detention in order to keep them from harm, or to the repulsive, bitter medicines that he might make them drink in order to put an end to their illness. Thus it is

stated in the Torah: *And you should consider in
your hearts that, as a man chastises his son, so the
Lord your God chastises you* (Deuteronomy, 8:5).
Scripture also says in regard to such matters: For
whom the Lord loves the Lord corrects, even as a
father the son in whom he delights (Proverbs,
3:12) (Saadia Gaon, *The Book of Beliefs and Opinions*, treatise 5, Chap. 3).

An intriguing dimension to the problem of
children's suffering is suggested in the legislation
concerning the wayward son. The Talmud has already established that it is primarily a theoretical
construct; that, in fact, the wayward son has never
existed and never will exist (*Sanhedrin* 71a).

With that preemptive caveat, the law of the
wayward son can be contemplated. The legislation
says, essentially, that if a son of two parents should
steal and eat a specific amount of meat and drink
a precise measure of a specific wine during the
three months immediately following the age of bar
mitzvah, and then is convicted of being a glutton
and a drunkard, he is stoned to death (see Deuteronomy 21:18–21).

Perhaps because so much within this runs contrary to our concept of justice, the Talmud insisted
that it could never happen. First, one does not become subject to the punitive measures of a court
until the age of twenty. Second, the death penalty
appears to be too severe for someone who has simply eaten or drunk in excess.

The rationale offered to explain this is that the
Torah projects a behavioral syndrome. The child
who has become involved in gluttonous activity

and needs to constantly reinforce the habit to which he has become addicted will be forced to steal to support the habit; and that eventually, in stealing, will meet with resistance and be forced to kill innocent people. Therefore, the Torah said, it is better for this person to die meritoriously rather than to die when actually deserving death.

Even this is inconsistent with the general approach that insists that we judge individuals not for what they will be, but rather for what they are. Ishmael, for example, was judged for what he was at the time (Genesis 21:17), even though his later behavior did not necessarily warrant such a positive judgment. Therefore, after all reasoning and explaining, it remains for us to search this legislation and to reap the benefits of our scrutiny.

The Torah here alerts families to a behavioral syndrome that can have drastic consequences. It anticipates, by many generations, the drug culture of the second half of the twentieth century. It asserts that bad habits can have drastic consequences and that therefore, there is an individual and a collective responsibility to stand on guard and be wary of such behavior patterns. If the patterns themselves are not capital crimes, they can certainly lead to the commission of capital crimes.

We are left to contemplate that, at times, a person is better off removed from this world and taken directly to the ultimate world. Only God knows when that time is.

More complicated and difficult to comprehend are statements in the Talmud, such as that a man's wife dies for his unfulfilled vows, or that children die as a punishment for the unfulfilled vows of the parent, not to mention a host of other reasons suggested for the death of children (*Shabbat* 32b).

Obviously, the death of someone close to one is perceived as a punishment to that person, who must endure the pain of having lost someone so precious. Most people's attention will be focused on the most obvious quandary: Why should innocent children die for the sins of their parents?

When children die at an early age, this does not mean that the children are being punished. This is in line with the famous talmudic comment that the persons who suffer the most in the passing of an individual are the survivors. The person who has died has gone to eternal rest, but those who survive are left in distress (*Mo'ed Katan* 25b).

It is as though adults are being told that if they do not act properly, if they make promises that they do not fulfill—which is a serious breach—they then forfeit their right either to marital bliss or to having a posterity. The hope of the rabbis undoubtedly was that people mend their behavior, so that the consequences that could accrue from this would not actually unfold.

The matter remains fraught with difficulty. It is not as though the rabbis are suggesting that every single death of a child occurs as a result of unfulfilled vows, or that any time a parent fails to fulfill a vow, that parent's child will die prematurely. The rabbis are suggesting that this may be the case in some instances. People should be careful, therefore, and should not be quick to blame God. In reality, it may be a human fault that precipitates the terrible calamity.

The general reaction to the terrible misfortune of losing a child is manifest in the sage Rabbi Abbahu, who had the misfortune to lose a young child. Rabbi Jonah and Rabbi Jose went to comfort him. Because of the awe in which they held him, they uttered no words of Torah to him. He asked them to say a word of Torah, but they asked him to do so. He said to them, "If for the government in this world, wherein there is lying, falsity, deceit, favoritism and taking of bribes, where one is here today and tomorrow is not, the relatives of a criminal who has been put to death greet the judges and the witnesses, saying—'We have no grudge against you in our hearts, for you have given a righteous judgement,' the government above, where there is no lying, falsity, deceit, favoritism and taking of bribes, where the judge is God Who lives and endures forever, how much more must we accept the administration of Justice" (Jerusalem Talmud, *Sanhedrin* 6:10).

This is not an easily assimilated attitude. The raw pain experienced upon the loss of a child is often too overwhelming to allow the approach of Rabbi Abbahu. But in the end, it is the only comfort: the conviction that what God has done, for whatever reason, will make ultimate sense. We and our children belong to God, and when an irreversible tragedy occurs, our task is to continue actualizing our responsibilities. Some acquire their world in one hour; some in many hours (*Avodah Zarah* 10b). Some people, including children, complete their mission earlier rather than later. Their death pains us less if we firmly believe that their passing, signifying "mission achieved," presages their entry into eternal life, where we hope to eventually meet them.

With all these important considerations, it is arrogant to conjecture that we can rationalize the pain and suffering of children any more than we can explain away the pain and suffering of adults. Once we believe we can do so, we forfeit a large part of our humanity. If we think we know the reason, we will think the suffering is justified, and therefore will have less sympathy for those in agony. It is a small step from there to human cruelty.

III

POINTING THE FINGER

6

In Our Hands

The obligation to affirm life by maintaining good health practices is one of the fundamental tenets of Judaism. Judaism places a great emphasis on self-preservation, on taking care of oneself, avoiding bad habits and dangerous practices that can compromise one's health or one's life. The full text of the verse that is often cited as the basis for this admonition is: "Be exceedingly heedful of yourself, for you saw no likeness at all on the day that God spoke to you in Horev out of the midst of the fire" (Deuteronomy 4:15).

The portion of the verse that suggests the precept of self-preservation is quite obvious. It inheres in the first part of the passage, admonishing the community, "Be exceedingly heedful of yourself." Notice that the imperative is not merely to be careful; it is to be *exceedingly* careful. Life is a precious gift, the most precious gift that God has entrusted to us. If we accept this gift with anything less than exceeding heed and special care, we thereby indicate a lack of appreciation for the monumental gift God has entrusted to us; we are derelict in a most fundamental way.

The remainder of the verse admonishing us to take care of ourselves remains quite perplexing. It seems to offer an explanation—namely, that we should do so because we saw no likeness of God when God appeared from out of the fire in Horev (Sinai) to transmit the Torah to the Israelite community.

What does one part of the verse have to do with the other? In what way is the obligation for self-preservation related to the fact that God did not appear in any form? This seems to be totally irrelevant to the obligation.

To gain a proper understanding of this passage, it is essential to reflect on the implication of the fact that God did not appear in a form. We know, as a basic theological principle, that God has no form. This is a clearly enunciated concept (Maimonides, *Laws of the Foundation of the Torah* 1:18).

However, even though God does not have any form or likeness, God may transmit a likeness to the people in order to project a particular message. The fact that the people perceive an arm of God intervening in a conflict or a voice of God transmitting a message does not automatically mean that God has an "arm" or a throat. In other words, what the people are shown is not necessarily what is. It is true that God has no shape or form; yet it is possible for the people to experience such a shape or form. This may occur simply because God desires it to occur.

However, at Sinai, when the commandments were given, God did not manifest any shape or form. The question that remains is: Why did God choose not to project any likeness? It is conceivable that God wanted to project a message by not appearing in any likeness. The people would not see any shape or experience any finite form; instead, they would perceive in the abstract.

God was thus telling the people that through what was transmitted to them, through their adherence to the commandments, they would give their lives the proper shape and form. In other words, God does not project finitude or absolutely nonnegotiable parameters. The people, through the way of life they espouse, can stretch any preconceived limits, or reduce them.

The verse is now more clear. We are told to be exceedingly heedful of ourselves. We are told that the length of one's life is not a finite, preordained number of years, but is rather a variable number of years, dependent on how we take care of ourselves. One person may have been allotted seventy or seventy-five years, but has abused life and may, therefore, live for a much shorter time; another person may have been allocated only forty-five or fifty years, but has carefully nurtured and respected that life, and therefore may exceed that allotted number of years. Taking care of ourselves makes sense only if the caretaking has a direct impact on the quantity and quality of our years. It is in this context that the balance of the passage should be understood.

We are to take heed of ourselves, to give our lives extended borders, because God chose not to appear in a finite shape. God chose to leave the shaping of our lives to us, as if to indicate that the destiny of our years is conditional upon how we take care of those years. We have no right to justify the abuse of our bodies by saying, *Vos is bashert is bashert* ("Whatever is destined is destined"). It is true that we may begin with some unknown destiny, but we can subtract from it or add to it depending on how we choose to live.

It may be difficult for us to comprehend, yet we must fully appreciate that God has effectively made us the custodians of our lives. Regarding the verse stating that the human being became a living species (Genesis 2:7), Rabbi Yehudah in the name of Rav states that God is thereby saying that "the soul that I have placed into you, you must give it life and sustain it" (*Taanit* 22b).

If we give our soul life we will sustain it, but if not, then ostensibly we will lose it. This comes directly from God. God has effectively revealed to us that we write our own story, that God has placed our destiny into our own hands.

The care that we are obliged to extend to ourselves is not only a spiritual care, but also a physical care. We cannot, and dare not, leave this to God. In fact, it is God who has told us that we must exercise this self-preservation. This is a Godly mandate, a mandate so strong that whenever there is a threat to life, Jewish law takes a back seat, in order to allow the quest for life to proceed unimpeded. Even though suffering may have beneficial end results if it is transmuted in a positive way, we are nevertheless obliged to avoid suffering, just as we are obliged to avoid illness.

It is not a value in and of itself to merely sit in misery; nor is it a value to seek out privations and physical tortures. If suffering comes upon one, and all efforts to alleviate the suffering are to no avail, then there is no choice but to endure in the best possible manner; but to fail to at least attempt to alleviate the suffering is theological folly. It flies in the face of the clear directive to be "exceedingly heedful" of ourselves (Deuteronomy 4:15). One who is suffering from an illness must search for a cure, and avail oneself of the cure if such is obtainable.

In addition, failure to do one's best to regain health runs contrary to the law that life-saving neutralizes serious obligations, including the obligation to preserve the Shabbat (*Shabbat* 132a).

We have been given the tools to achieve self-preservation. These tools are God's directive that we must do so, and God's further directive that almost all other Godly directives are suspended in the exercise of self-preservation.

"R. Aha states: 'And God will remove from you all illness' (Deuteronomy 7:15)—It is from you that illness should not befall you [i.e., it is in our hands]" (*Midrash Rabbah*, Leviticus 16:8). R. Aha indicates that the fact that we have been given the tools implies that our health is in our hands. This is not a sacrilegious comment, for it is God who has

placed our health in our hands. We have the tools—
and the responsibility.

Generally, the law of cause-and-effect applies
to the way we take care of ourselves. Those who
take care will have a better quality of life, and will
live longer. Those who are neglectful will usually
suffer the natural consequences of neglect.

This is in the nature of a covenant between
God and the people. A covenant is a two-way street.
It involves an if–then relationship. If party number one will do so-and-so, then party number two
will respond with such-and-such.

This covenantal relationship is established at
the very outset of B'hukkotai. Israel is told, "If you
walk in My statutes and keep My commandments
and do them, then I will give your rains in their
season and the land shall yield its produce, and
the trees of the field shall yield their fruit . . . and
you shall eat your bread to satisfaction and you
will dwell in your land in tranquility" (Leviticus
26:3–5).

At first glance, this seems to be a covenantal
agreement. If the people follow God's word, then
they will be rewarded with bountiful yield, which
they will enjoy in tranquility.

As welcome an arrangement as this may seem,
it appears to be contrary to the basic principle,
"There is no reward for the fulfillment of the precepts in this world" (*Kiddushin* 31b). If the aforementioned covenant is taken as a reward, then it
is a blatant contradiction of the idea that there is
no reward for the fulfillment of the precepts in
this world. The covenant states clearly that there

is a reward, a very tangible reward at that, for the fulfillment of the precepts.

Concerning the promise that you will "eat your bread to satisfaction," Rashi, quoting *Torat Kohanim*, states that you will eat a little bit, but it will be blessed in your digestive system. This observation offers a hint as to the nature of what seems to be a covenantal affirmation.

The blessing is not one of bountiful yield. It is more a blessing of quality than of quantity. The little bit that you eat will be to satisfaction; it will not be necessary to have an abundance of food in order to feel satisfied.

There will be blessing, but it will be related to the people's mindset. They will not be on a gluttonous path; they will eat in a value-imbued way. Instead of consuming whatever they can, they will share with others and will be satisfied with what little they do eat. This is the Torah concept of ideal consumption.

We are to be concerned not just with ourselves, but with the environment around us. We have no right to assume that the land is ours, and that we can therefore abuse it without consideration of the consequences of that abuse. We must be sure to give the land its rest in the sabbatical year. We must, at the same time, see to it that the have-nots of the community are well-provided-for through our bounty.

People who are "outer-oriented," whose concern is for fulfilling values and transcending their selves, are much less likely to be narcissistic. Their needs are minimal, and they will be satisfied with little; they will thus have plenty to share with others less fortunate. This is alluded to in the first part of the covenant, namely, "If you will follow My statutes and observe My precepts and do them . . . ." Actualizing this in its all-embracing implication leads to the ultimate of blessings, the blessing of a community that is fortunate to have caring citizens who concern themselves with the welfare of the populace.

What God is hereby introducing is not so much a reward for adherence to the precepts as the spelling out of a cause and effect. The effect of individuals abiding by all the laws—laws to protect the ecology and the people within that ecological system—is that you have tranquility. You will be able to enjoy whatever yield is forthcoming from the field and the trees. The serenity will come from living in a society wherein the poor appreciate that the wealthy have not cut them off, but are deeply concerned about them. The poor will then not attack them, despoil them, or be envious of them. The trees in the field will bear fruit because those responsible for eliciting the agricultural capacity do so in a sensitive manner.

The reward for adherence to covenant is not a this-worldly reward. In this world, there are only legitimate consequences, and good ones at that, for living a life of good deeds and responsible behavior. To be satisfied with a little is to be satisfied a lot.

On this theme of eating less and having more left to share with others, consider the far-reaching statement of Maimonides that most illnesses come

upon a person either because of eating bad foods
or because of stuffing oneself in a gross fashion
even with foods that are naturally good (Maimonides, *Mishnah Torah*, Laws of Tendencies [*De'ot*]
4:15).

Maimonides goes so far as to guarantee (ibid.
4:20) that whoever watches the self, and eats properly and behaves properly, that person will not
know of illness until becoming older, and will not
need a doctor unless the body was not healthy
from the start, or if one previously, earlier in life,
adopted bad habits, or if a plague or famine visits
itself upon the world.

Maimonides (*Mishnah Torah*, Laws of Tendencies [*De'ot*] 4:1) postulates that a healthy and complete body is in the category of Godly affirmations,
since being sick is not conducive to gaining a true
knowledge of God. Therefore it is imperative that
one distance the self from anything that is destructive to the body.

But there are always apparent exceptions to
the rule, like the twenty-year-old athlete who suddenly collapses or the obese smoker who lives to
a ripe old age. When such exceptions come to our
attention, we tend to question whether it is worthwhile to follow the rules and guidelines. This is
somewhat related to the concomitant tendency to
see the exception as the representative reality,
rather than seeing the exception for what it is—an
aberration that may have a deeper explanation.

But questioning whether taking care is worthwhile is akin to questioning whether one must be
sober when driving, since some drivers who are

royally drunk actually do arrive at their destinations without incident. There are exceptions to the most sensible of rules, but the exceptions do not compromise the rules.

What is true of the purely physical—medical and health components of choice—is also true of the spiritual. There are specific linkages between spiritual options and longevity, be they linkages of quantity or of quality.

For example, the Talmud reports a dialogue between Rav Ada the son of Ahavah, and his students, who asked their teacher, "To what do you attribute your longevity?" Rav Ada responded with a full array of spiritually imbued behaviors, beginning with, "In all my life I never stood on ceremony in my own household" (*Taanit* 20b). This is an element of righteousness: not insisting on the continuing affirmation of one's importance, and instead exhibiting genuine humility.

Anger is considered a behavior pattern that is not consistent with good health, such that, in the view of Rabbe Yonatan, one who is prone to or habituated to anger will be dominated by all types of hellish manifestations (*Nedarim* 22a). All types of bodily afflictions will overcome the individual. This is another instance of the fact that our health is directly related to our habits, for better or for worse.

Ben Sira (Ecclesiasticus 31) advises that "a heart that is anxious will age prematurely." Being full of anxiety, and tending towards depression because of the severity of that anxiety, is not conducive to longevity; living a life of joy is conducive to longevity. Since longevity is an essential desire, it obviously means that we must cultivate the character traits and habits that contribute to that longevity.

Here, too, there are no hard and fast guarantees; nor should there be guarantees. If it were guaranteed that every single individual who behaved in a righteous and health-preserving manner would have a long, healthful, and fulfilling life, and other individuals who did the opposite would have a short, curtailed life, then, effectively, free choice would be denied us.

We would not have any more free choice because we would choose the good not because of its being a free exercise of one's will toward virtue, but simply because it is the more prudent way to be. Midrash, on the verse, "And God saw everything which God had made, and behold it was very good" (Genesis 1:31), questions why death befalls the righteous, and responds that "it had to befall the righteous too, or else the wicked might have said, 'The righteous live because they practice the Law and good works: We will do so too,' and they would have fulfilled the commandments deceitfully, and not for their own sake" (*Genesis Rabbah* 9:5-9).

Choosing righteousness out of prudence, instead of choosing righteousness for its own sake, is not what God designed for human affirmation. We are asked to live righteously, and the world's reality is so designed that we should choose righteousness for its own sake, and not make this choice based on the rewards that may accrue from the decision. Ultimately, righteousness must be perceived as its own reward.

At the same time, it is illogical to assume that there is no recompense for doing that which is right. A world run so haphazardly certainly would not fit in with an ordered universe that was created by God, and ultimately is subject to God's verdict. Within a specifically prescribed framework, there is a sense to the world. Those who exercise usually live longer, those who eat better usually have fewer illnesses, those who take better care of their bodies generally are in better vigor. But there is always the exception that throws everything off rhythm, the aforementioned exercise fiend who suddenly collapses and dies, or the corpulent smoker who lives well into his eighties. These give us pause, and lead us to question our own cause-and-effect relationship between good choices and good results.

But for individuals to retain freedom—that is, the freedom to make a choice based on righteousness for its own sake, as opposed to functioning in a world that is governed entirely by cause and effect, we must have these exceptions.

7

The Harsh Reality

The exercise of freedom makes all individuals vulnerable to the consequences of the free and sometimes malevolent choices of others. However, there is illness and sickness in the world that seems just to be there, as if ordained by God, and having no relationship to the behavior of human beings towards each other. The question that arises is why we must contend with this type of suffering. Ultimately, we do not know the answer to this or to any other question related to suffering. We fumble around for a rationale, but the bottom line is that ultimate explanations are beyond us.

However, a possible hint at a response to this question is the famous statement in the Jerusalem Talmud that out of 100 individuals who die prematurely, 99 die as a result of negligence (*Shabbat* 14:3). Korban HaEydah explains the negligence is that they are not careful regarding cold and heat, excessive eating and promiscuousness, and anger (loc. cit.).

In simple arithmetic, 99 percent of all premature deaths are our fault, and one percent is God's fault. Is it not possible that God, seeing the explosion of negligence on the world, simply says to the world at large, "If you insist, through negligence, in bringing plague on this world, then why should I go out of my way for you? I want you to come back to me and say—'Why have you done this,' because then I can say to you—'Why have you done that?'"

We have no right to demand of God what we, as a collective entity, are not prepared to demand of ourselves. We know what it takes to be healthy; we know what to stay away from in order to avoid illness. By not doing so, we are thumbing our collective noses at God—and then we beg for God's mercy. That, in simple terms, is *hutzpah* (arrogance). God may respond favorably to our *hutzpah*, but that is an extraordinary kindness that must be appreciated as much more than a deserved reward.

The ratio of 99 to 1 is overwhelmingly disproportionate, but the 1 is a very important percentage. It is God's way of awakening people to the evil that they are perpetuating by their behavior. This is one possibility, amongst others, that may explain the reality of certain types of suffering.

The message of this rather harsh explanation is quite clear: The overwhelming majority of premature deaths occur because of our own negligence. Before we rush to complain to God about what God has wrought, we must do a bit of self-investigation and must answer for the 99 out of the 100 that are directly attributable to human negligence.

What do you make of the following situation, which I confronted a number of years ago? A man who smoked three packs of cigarettes a day told me, one terrible morning, in the midst of violent coughing, that his doctor had just told him that he had inoperable lung cancer, and that he had no chance of survival. Crushed and angry, he uttered those words that are so painful to hear but, in some circumstances, are so understandable: "Why is God doing this to me? Why is God punishing me? I have been such a good person all my life."

I did not have the heart to tell this man that if you smoke three packs of cigarettes a day and you live to be sixty-five, that is a miracle, and you should be thanking God that you have lasted this long. I could not tell him that, even though I wanted to. But how do we justify complaining to God if we really cannot defend our claim on longevity because we simply have not given our health the care that it demands?

In his classic work, *Emunot V'Deot*, Rabbenu Saadia speaks about the pains with which the soul is afflicted because of its connection with the body, and that these pains are due to one of two causes:

> If, for example, they are aches that it has contracted by exposure at the time of darkness or of excessive heat or cold, the fault is its own and not that of its Master. For He has endowed the soul with intelligence and enjoined it to beware of such evils, but it disregards the injunction . . . .

On the other hand, if these pains have been brought upon it by its Master, the only possible explanation, in view of God's justice and mercy, is that He permitted them to come upon it as a discipline in order that He might, in return therefor, requite the soul with good. This is borne out by such statements of Scripture as; *That He might afflict thee, and that He might prove thee, to do thee good at thy latter end* (Deuteronomy, 8:16) (*The Book of Beliefs and Opinions*, translated by Samuel Rosenblatt, New Haven: Yale University Press, 1948, Treatise 6, Chap. 4, pp. 249–250).

One may assume that Saadia would place those who are exposed to heat or cold for lack of shelter in the second category, as suffering not from choice but as a result of divine visitation.

Control of sexual behavior is considered vital to the health of the world. Midrash Tanhuma suggests that plagues come upon the world because of sexual promiscuity (*Tazria* 1). People who embark on destructive paths thereby damage their own well-being and the well-being of innocent others. This is not merely a twentieth-century phenomenon; it is part of the human condition. At any point in history, illicit behavior usually begets illicit results.

However, there is more to prevention than simply maintaining tight moral standards. For example, Isi son of Judah addresses the question of why the talmudic Sages died prematurely. He responds that it is not because they are sexually promiscuous, not because they rob, but because they despise themselves—i.e., they are negligent in the care of themselves (*Avot D'Rabbe Natan* 29:6). Apparently, the Sages would sit through the talmudic discourses of their teachers even when they needed to visit the privy. This engendered intestinal disorders that compromised their longevity. The Talmud goes on to state that if a person dies from this type of illness (intestinal disorders), it is a good sign—i.e., a sign that the person probably was a righteous individual (*Ketuvot* 103b).

A host of regulations exists regarding health preservation and good health habits. Consider the talmudic advice that a person about to have a meal should make sure that the body is clean. This is achieved by walking back and forth a few times and then relieving oneself of any internal excess, and only then sitting down to eat (*Shabbat* 82a).

Health preservation includes avoiding that which is dangerous. For example, it was forbidden for people to drink from streams and from swamps both by mouth and by hand, and those that did so were responsible for their own death because of the danger involved in such practice (*Avodah Zarah* 12b).

The Sages had a good understanding of the importance of the evacuatory system, stating that difficulties in evacuation are as painful and as difficult to a person as the day of the person's demise (*Pesahim* 118a). Rabbi Judah was once told that his robust face was reminiscent of someone who lent money on interest or who raised pigs. He said that both of these activities were forbidden and that he had nothing to do with them, but that there were twenty-four privies between his house and the talmudic academy, and on his way to the academy, he would make use of every privy to ensure that his intestinal system was cleaned out; that was why he looked so healthful (*Berakhot* 55a).

Holding oneself in, not releasing the internal excess when the body says that the time has arrived, is considered a prohibition under the general rubric of "Do not abominate yourselves" (Leviticus 20:25) (*Makkot* 16b). Rabbi Hiyya advises that one who wants to avoid intestinal difficulties should be sure not to restrain the self when the need to evacuate is pressing (*Gittin* 70a).

A Sage is not permitted to live in any city that lacks certain things, including a privy and a doctor. According to Rabbi Akiva, the city must even have a good supply of fruits (*Sanhedrin* 17b). "Who is a wealthy individual?" asks Rabbi Yosi. Whoever has a privy or a bathroom close to the table (*Shabbat* 25a). Aside from the obvious meaning, this is also a reflection on the delicate balance people must maintain.

There is a pervasive feeling amongst the Sages that overeating and eating poorly are quite detrimental to health. In this regard, Rava states (*Shabbat* 33a) that more people die from overeating than from undereating—or, in more precise language, "more people are killed by the pot than are blown up by famine."

The excess food that humans consume goes to waste; worse yet, it has a deleterious effect on the body. Having your bathroom close to your dining-room table, metaphorically speaking, is meant to remind you to be especially careful not to overeat.

Preventive medicine is preferable to curative medicine. We are urged, "Honor your doctor before you need the doctor" (Jerusalem Talmud, *Taanit* 3:6). The Talmud, reflecting the values of the Torah, contains a massive array of regulations regarding health care. Good medicine is good Judaism, because it reflects our acute awareness that health is God's gift to us. Failure to nurture that gift is therefore a sacrilege and, in a sense, a failure to recognize a primary article of faith.

The Talmud reports a dialogue between Alexander the Great and the Sages of the Negev (*Tamid* 32a). Alexander asked the Sages: "What should a person do in order to live?" The Sages responded: "Let the person reflect upon his or her mortality." Alexander asked further: "What should a person do in order to die?" The Sages responded: "Let the person overindulge [technically, this refers to raising one's self-importance and thereby arousing the envy of others]."

This is the paradox of life—that, to the extent we realize that we are mortal and finite and that we therefore live our lives within our boundaries and within our limits, we will thus enhance our lives. However, if we overindulge and wallow in self-importance, then this overindulgence will be our undoing. It is clear that how we live, and, therefore, how long we live, is, to a large extent, under our control.

A profound number of insights on the issue of suffering as it relates to our own behavior come from the classic Jewish ethical treatise, *Pirkay Avot* (Ethics of the Elders). There, in a wide-ranging Mishnah, we are instructed as to the far-reaching consequences of our ethical behavior.

We have already pointed out the view of the Sages regarding the pervasive effect of sexual promiscuity. The implications of such behavior, and the adverse consequences deriving therefrom, go beyond the immediate participants. Deviant ethical behavior, the failure to live up to one's fundamental ethical responsibilities, likewise has far-reaching consequences. The Mishnah states:

> Seven kinds of calamity come upon the world for seven types of transgression: 1) If some give their tithes and others do not, famine from drought ensues, some suffer hunger while some are satiated; 2) if all decide not to give tithes, famine through panic and drought ensues; 3) if all decide not to set apart the dough-offering, an all-consuming famine ensues; 4) pestilence comes upon the world for the commission of those capital crimes enumerated in the Torah, the punishments for which were not turned over to a human court, and for violations of the law concerning produce of the sabbatical year; 5) the sword comes upon the world for the delay of justice, for the perversion of justice, and for those who teach the Torah inconsistent with its true interpretation; 6) wild beasts come upon the world because of vain swearing and the desecration of God's name; 7) exile comes upon the world because of idolatry, immorality, murder, and violation of the law concerning the rest for the soil in the sabbatical year (*Avot* 5:11).

This Mishnah deals, at least in the first parts, with those who are overly concerned with materialistic matters and exceed acceptable norms in their attempt to gain wealth. The Mishnah indicates that there is an element of consequence to all human action, especially when dealing with dereliction of responsibility toward others. This usually bounces back to the perpetrators of the crime of miserliness.

If some give their tithes and others do not, there is mirrorlike reaction in which there is a drought famine, where some people go hungry but others do not. Those who refuse to give their tithes are stingy, unwilling to share with the Levites and the poor. Their tendency toward material possessions results in hoarding, in over-working the earth, in too much expectation. Even in the natural order of things, this leads to a destruction of the earth's propensities.

If all decide not to give tithes, then a worse type of famine ensues, one that involves panic. Those who are dependent upon the tithes obviously do not have what they need, and those who have refused to give them are constantly searching for more. This leads to a panic situation.

If all decide not to set apart the dough-offering, then the ensuing famine is an all-consuming one. Dough-offering, referred to as the taking of *hallah,* involves a minute amount of *hallah.* If there is stinginess even in the giving of *hallah,* then these miserly individuals are probably working the land to death and, by their insensitivity, bringing about the starvation of those who are in need of their help.

Pestilence comes upon the world for those crimes committed that are not given to a human court for judgment. Those who perpetrate such crimes know full well that no human court can judge them; they feel free to challenge the enforceability of the law. In fact, they are right; the law cannot be enforced. They can claim, for example, that the fruits of the seventh year were collected legitimately when, in fact, they had not left them for others, as they were obliged to do.

All these are transgressions wherein it might be assumed that there is no ultimate court that can exact payment and bring to justice those who have perpetrated these elusive crimes. However, the Mishnah indicates that pestilence will evolve from the proliferation of these actions, pestilence being a type of hidden disease that causes damage in a way commensurate with the nature of the crimes. The crimes were performed stealthily, in an attempt to elude the force of law. The force of law shows itself to be stronger still, and sends the type of plague from which one cannot escape.

The delay of justice, the perversion of justice, and the existence of those who teach the Torah *inconsistent with its true interpretation,* distorting the instrument of the Jewish legal system—all of these contribute to a chaos that is possible only when justice and the comprehension of the law are not given their proper expression. In chaos, individuals will lift up *swords.* There will be a destruction that comes from the nonenforcement of the legal statutes.

Vain swearing and the desecration of God's Name bring wild beasts upon the world. Humankind has many responsibilities, but the most basic one is to acknowledge God's Creation of the world and God's sanctity. Vain swearing, which is the unnecessary use of God's Name and its desecration, are base expressions of depraved individuals who have rejected even this fundamental notion of God's sanctity.

Such people have, by so doing, reduced human beings to animals. They do not subscribe to the idea of the sanctity of God. There is no sanctity of Creation, and, hence, no uniqueness of the human being. People are simply two-legged animals; in keeping with this, they will be visited by their brethren, the wild beasts.

The land of Israel, which was given to the people of Israel, was seen as the breeding ground of a higher system of ethics, one in which idolatry would be impossible, immorality nonexistent, and murder unheard-of. The land was to be treated differently from other lands; it was to be seen as sacred unto God, and therefore a rest was to be given to it on the seventh year. These are the basic ingredients that justify existence in the land of Israel. When these conditions do not obtain, then *exile* is the result, because there is no legitimate spiritual lifestyle that justifies the granting of the land in the first place.

This Mishnah establishes a clear line of cause-and-effect for all our behavior, spanning the vast expanse of the moral and the ethical. These rules of consequence are firm warnings that what we do spills over beyond our own immediate world. These rules are therefore a plea to be careful, and to be caring. Ultimately, the poverty and disease caused by the delinquency of the rich will return to haunt the rich.

All of this does not resolve some of the critical issues that are obvious to us. Why is it that people who apparently take care of themselves and seem to do everything right, from diet to exercise to general lifestyle, are stricken with diseases? Why is it that most people who receive blood transfusions are helped, but a few receive tainted blood that may kill them? Why is it that some people who seem to take no care of themselves are perfectly healthy?

We do not have the answers to these questions, nor should we expect to. In general, life conforms to the law of averages and the principles of logic. On a logical basis, those who exercise regularly, eat properly, get the right amount of sleep, and so forth, are the ones most likely to live longer, whereas those who overindulge and who squander away life are more likely to suffer the consequences. This is how it should be.

There will always be the odd circumstance that destroys this hard-and-fast rule. The fact that there is no absolute cause-and-effect relationship is part and parcel of life's equation. Basically, we are individuals with free will who are urged to use our free will in a positive manner.

It is in the very nature of our freedom of choice that we may make the wrong choices or the right ones. However, in order for us to make enlightened choices, the general rules of probability have to prevail. We are aware that all rules of probability have exceptions, but if there were no rules and everything was random, with no link between taking care of oneself and the positive consequences emanating therefrom, then we would not merely be denied free choice; worse still, we would not know how to choose.

8

Kashrut and Health

A word is in order about the rules of *kashrut* (the full scope of foods that are permitted or forbidden), which occupy much space in the Torah and the Talmud, and which take up a large segment of the Jewish agenda.

It is folly to suggest that the rules of *kashrut* are all health-motivated. Once we do that, we are in danger of putting too much stock in "new" medical discoveries showing that foods that are purportedly bad for one's health are actually good, or that foods deemed healthful are now considered detrimental to health, and so on. Should that happen, one will then question, and perhaps even renounce, the biblical prescription.

However, it is not out of bounds to suggest that the restrictions that fall under the broad category of *kashrut* do have a health component to them, and that one of the collateral benefits of

adhering to the kosher code is that good health
will accrue therefrom. Actually, suggesting otherwise would make little sense. The Torah, as we
have seen, operates within the context of concern
for self-preservation, and postulates principles
and guidelines for taking good care of ourselves.
At the very least, therefore, the Torah would not
suggest any observance or dietary code that is
injurious to health. Most likely, if a code is to be
suggested, it will be conducive to good health.

Consistent with this notion, Nahmanides suggests that a reason permitted fish must have fins
and scales is that these help create a warmer inte-
rior and a more even distribution of the vital matter within, thus making the fish more wholesome
(Nahmanides, Leviticus 11:10).

The animals that are prohibited—animals that
are wild and prey on other animals, like the birds
of prey (see Nahmanides, Leviticus 11:13)—are likewise hot-blooded and do not digest their food, but
rather swallow it, much as they devour other animals. Kosher animals, on the other hand, have
ruminating stomachs; because of this they digest
their food and spread it out evenly over the body,
thus affording better nutrition for the human
being (Rabbi Aharon of Barcelona, *Sefer HaHinukh*,
nos. 73, 147, and 154). This is not why we observe
the kosher code, although it is a beneficial side
effect of adhering to the kosher regulations.

The *halakhah* (Jewish law) of self-preservation
stipulates that one must avoid such dangers as a
rickety wall that is about to fall (*Yoreh De'ah* 116:5;
see *Rosh HaShanah* 16b, *Taanit* 20b), and to absent

oneself from a city where there is plague and pestilence, for fear that one will fall into its grip.

Medical treatment is considered an essential part of life, and of life-affirmation. It is not surprising, therefore, that the Talmud, which discusses the most important spiritual issues, also has some very practical medical advice. One classic example is the listing (*Gittin* 70a), of those things that are of medical benefit to the person, and those things that may actually bring on illness. To be healthy and, therefore, be able to serve God is in itself a primary religious value.

Maimonides (*Mishnah Torah*, Laws of Ceasing and Desisting on the Tenth [the Laws of Yom Kippur] 2:8), states that if a person who is dangerously ill has asked to eat on Yom Kippur, even though the doctor says that the patient does not need this food, we feed the patient according to the patient's own assessment until the person says that he or she has had enough. If the expert doctor states that the patient needs to eat, even though the patient does not wish to, we feed the patient anyway. We err on the side of life.

Judaism is generally life-affirming in all its dimensions. This means that the individual is urged to enjoy all the bounties of life that God has provided for us. One is not to engage in deprivation and denial as if it were a value in its own right. Generally, one is excused from the actualization of a commandment if it will endanger life (*Yoma* 85b). Danger to life suspends the affirmative code of Jewish existence. According to some (Maimonides, *Mishnah Torah*, Laws of the Foundations of

Torah 5:4), this does not even allow one the possibility of being a theological hero. One must suspend religious observance for the higher reality—life itself.

The principle of life-affirmation is thus quite pervasive, going far beyond the diet and touching many aspects of life. In all this, God's prescriptive desire for our individual and collective well-being comes through quite strongly. Any questions we have of God must be asked in full awareness of God's desire.

9

Questioning Ourselves

Suffering is a term that we tend to associate with serious intrusion on one's physical well-being or emotional tranquility; yet the talmudic understanding of suffering embraces a wide range of contingencies. The definition of one who is suffering as a result of divine visitation includes a person whose shirt was turned inside out (*Arakhin* 16b), or one who wanted to remove three coins from the pocket and pulled out only two (the person must return to the pocket to get more money).

In this far-reaching concept, a wide range of disappointments or unfulfilled desires is included in the category of suffering. We all would prefer an inside-out shirt to a life that has been turned inside-out by tragedy. However, the momentary frustration of someone who is in a hurry and whose inside-out shirt causes unwelcome delay is not a trivial matter at the time.

Anything that disappoints us, stops us in our tracks, and forces us out of our life pattern is a jolt that merits being categorized as suffering. These jolts, however small, are signals. At least, we are urged to see them as signals, as wake-up calls to reorder our priorities. Since we all need these periodic awakenings, it is obviously preferable to be awakened with a relatively benign nudge, but we usually do not recognize that we are being awakened until the jolt is quite severe.

When we are jolted, our immediate reflex is to ask, "Why?" Some get more personal, and ask: "Why me?" The "why" question needs to be addressed on a general level and on a personal level. On the general level, we need to appreciate our own severe limitations—our inability to apprehend the full nature, design, and purpose of God's agenda.

Rabbi Eliezer Papo, in his classic work, *Pele Yoetz*, quotes the Talmud's dictum (*Hagigah* 13a) that we should not try to question those things that are beyond us (p. 262). We can ask why, and we can even intend this question on the general level; but we should not engage in intricate inquiry, as if we expect to learn the answer to a question that was posed by Moses, for which he did not receive the answer.

The "response" that Moses received was, "The righteous person who enjoys prosperity is perfectly righteous; the righteous person who is afflicted with adversity is not perfectly righteous. The wicked person who enjoys prosperity is not perfectly wicked; the wicked person who is afflicted with adversity is perfectly wicked" (*Berakhot*

7a). This is simply a retrospective response; we still do not know who qualifies for which category.

Beyond that, Rabbi Meir claims that when God said, "I will be gracious to whom I will be gracious" (Exodus 33:19), God meant that the person may not be deserving; "and I will show mercy on whom I will show mercy" likewise means that the person may not be deserving (ibid.). In other words, we do not even have general retrospective parameters.

With regard to the suffering that comes at the hands of others, Rabbi Papo suggests that even if evil has come to a person through the actions of other bad individuals—who will have to face judgment because their evil was exercised by their own free will—nevertheless, the afflicted person should realize that what happened was probably the result of something he or she did wrong (p. 262).

In *Pele Yoetz*, Rabbi Papo (p. 262) quotes the Talmud (*Berakhot* 5a)—that those who sense that affliction is being visited upon them should search their own deeds. *Pele Yoetz* refers to a person who was in awe of God and so far removed from wrongdoing that when he suffered any losses in business dealings or lost any of his possessions, he would run from the marketplace to his home to engage in soul-searching, repent, and lament that whatever happened was a result of his wrongdoing.

Rabbi Papo goes on to say, however, that today, lamentably, no one takes this to heart, and people like to attribute whatever occurs to some natural circumstance. This illness came because of such-and-such a reason, this loss came because of that

circumstance, and no one takes to heart the necessity for self-investigation and repentance. Even
those who try to comfort the afflicted offer explanations such as, "This is the way of the world";
"There is evil in the world"; "Many have imbibed
from the cup of suffering." No one says, however,
that these afflictions are a result of one's sin.

Rabbi Papo is astute enough to realize that it
would be improper to say this. If one actually tells
a person that this affliction is a punishment for
his or her sins, then instead of giving comfort,
one will instead increase the other person's pain,
thereby causing enmity between them. Indeed,
conveying such a sentiment to a suffering person
is prohibited, according to Jewish law (*Shulhan
Arukh*, Hoshen Mishpat 228:4).

Pele Yoetz concludes (p. 263) with the suggestion that one who sees affliction coming should
try with all one's strength to give up at least one
action that is not good, and embrace at least one
good deed that previously was not effected, as a
way of improvement in reaction to the suffering,
which obviously did not come by accident.

As to the agonizing question of why God has
caused this suffering (the Yiddish version of this
lament, *Far voss hut mir Gott geshtroft*, has a more
piercing impact), those pondering it should never
forget a most crucial scriptural verse: "For whom
the Lord loves, the Lord rebukes, as a father the
son whom he favors" (Proverbs 3:12).

It seems clear and generally accepted, from
various Torah and talmudic sources, that illness,
suffering, and affliction are all Godly visitations on

a person that result mainly as a consequence of the person's mistakes or sins.

Much as we would like to reject such a proposition, it is an inescapable part of Jewish tradition. The question that arises is, "Now that we have this proposition before us, what do we make of it?"

It is intellectually dishonest to reject this inescapable and harsh declaration with the disingenuous claim that it is not part of Jewish tradition. It is ineluctably part of Jewish tradition, and it behooves us to wrestle with it and to understand it in its full implications. Such arguments as "God did not (or could not, or would not) do it," however fancifully convincingly presented, are nothing more than theological gibberish.

Those looking for an easy out or wanting to avoid a serious confrontation with their own behavior will welcome such gibberish. It sounds better, it is more emotionally reassuring—at least superficially—and circumvents the need to make any significant lifestyle changes.

What do we make of the assumption, for example, that illness and suffering are the result of a person's sins? We should not take this as suggesting a negative judgment of the individual. Who amongst us can claim to be perfect? The fact that a person has sinned is in no way to be construed as a judgment about the quality of that person.

We are all imperfect, and this imperfection is a direct result of our being human. This does not diminish our righteousness. "For there is no righteous individual on earth who does good and will not sin" (Ecclesiastes 7:20).

Our capacity for evil makes all our good actions our choice, uniquely our deed, and, therefore, laudable. But the flip side of accolades for good deeds is blame and consequence for wrongdoing. If we refuse to accept blame, we must also refuse to accept praise. But the dialectic is usually one-sided: "Praise me, but do not blame me."

It is possible for one to commit some wrongs in life and still be a very righteous person. The question that many people raise when they are going through the agony of suffering, *Far voss hut mir der Eybeshter geshtroft?* (Why has God punished me?) is haunting. It is pertinent if meant as a serious question, not as it is usually intended—as a complaint or lament.

No rabbi on pastoral rounds would dare to say to a patient, "Well, God has punished you, and obviously because you deserve it." This is insensitive, counterproductive, and legally prohibited, even if it may be true (see further on this, Chapter 30). It is not for others to impose this sense of guilt and wrongdoing on the afflicted person. It is better for sufferers to appreciate this on their own, and to anticipate the untoward eventualities before they are ill.

Self-rebuke that goes straight to the heart is better for the individual than a hundred lashes (*Berakhot* 7a). This is much easier to integrate into one's psyche when healthy, in order to plan in advance for how one will later react to illness.

We must utterly reject the psychojargon of recent years that goes to extraordinary lengths to protect the fragile egos of contemporary folk. Purveyors of such goods would be horrified at the prospect of suggesting to a suffering person, however delicately, that he or she may be at fault.

We must disabuse ourselves of the notion that we are perfect, that we can do no wrong, and that we are not deserving of any blame. This notion is destructive even in good health, as it will undoubtedly interfere with any growth process. It is also a serious impediment to forging any meaningful relationships.

In illness, unable as we are to fully fathom God's intentions for us, we can, and should, embrace the opportunity to engage in genuine introspection. We ought to question ourselves.

We ought to be mindful of the observation that "One's foolishness corrupts the way but the heart rages against God (Proverbs 19:3). Rashi comments that this refers to our tendency to blame God for consequences that are brought on by our own behavior.

Blaming God gets us nowhere and obstructs any meaningful self-examination. But self-examination is where the action should be.

IV

HOW TO FIGHT

10

Thinking About Illness in Health

A wit once remarked that he was not afraid of dying; he just did not want to be there when it happened.

Well, it happens to all of us, and we are there when it happens. Most people are less afraid of dying than they are of how they will die. They do not want protracted illness, excruciating pain, debilitating infirmity, or loss of primary physical and mental function.

The aging process is a source of worry. If only there were a way to grow older gracefully, and to maintain the most fundamental human capacities. "Remember your Creator in the days of your youth, before the bad days come, and the years arrive when you will say—I have no desire for them" (Ecclesiastes 12:1). *"The bad days,"* says the Talmud, refers to older age; *"and the years arrive when you will say—I have no desire for them"* refers to suffering (*Shabbat* 151b). Herein is expressed the dread of aging and the complications associated with the aging process.

Therefore, states Rabbi Aba, people should pray for a good old age, that they should have sight and that they should be able to eat and drink, and walk, because normally when a person gets old, these capacities depart and the person is no longer able to do these things (*Tanhuma*, Mikketz 10).

The prayer for a good old age must be initiated long before old age creeps in; by then, prayer is too late. Praying earlier on for a dignified and fulfilling old age means more than just adding a further supplication to one's list of entreaties: This prayer also establishes a focus on the future, and reminds those asking for God's help that they must do their part if they expect God to help them.

The part we play in the unfolding of our older age relates to how we integrate a number of basic ideas into our lifestyle from the earliest stages. The first idea is that we should look upon health as a precious gift from God to be nurtured and sanctified, not squandered or cavalierly disregarded. We carry out this nurturing by adhering to the health guidelines of the Torah and the Talmud, guidelines that incorporate dietary as well as psychological concerns.

Second, the appreciation of good health as a gift ought also to take into account what strategies the individual will employ when that great gift is diminished or even taken away. Strategic long-term planning is appropriate not only in terms of saving for retirement, but also in terms of making plans for the inevitabilities of life. The wise person anticipates the future (*Avot* 4:1).

It is interesting the way our lives work—or, more accurately, the way we work our lives. We plan for everything except illness. We plan for retirement with retirement programs; we also plan for after we have passed from this world by making detailed wills discussing what should happen after we die; we even create living wills or instructions specifying what should be done for us or to us if we permanently lose our mental capacity. We do very little planning, however, for the interim between retirement and our imminent demise. We do not think about what we will do when our capacities are limited and we are not the same as we were before. This is lamentable. As difficult as such planning may be, it would make this transition so much more smooth.

Although it would be ridiculous to suggest that such planning would make the transition totally smooth, nevertheless it would be an improvement over coming into this new situation without any idea about what is to be done or how one is to react.

The most important rule of thumb about what we plan to do when we are slowed down by the inevitable life progression is that whatever pattern we establish for ourselves in our vibrant years is not likely to change dramatically in our later years.

I recall many people who have reassured me, independent of my prodding, that things would be different when they retired. "Don't worry, Rabbi— after I retire, you will see me in *shul* regularly." I am still waiting.

Nor can someone who did absolutely no study-
ing in the peak years of adulthood expect that suddenly, after a lengthy hiatus, the brain and the
heart will be ready for intellectual stimulation. It
is not impossible, but it is also not very likely. It is
important to be able to study in one's later years,
if for no other reason than to be able to wake up
every morning with a sense of purpose, rather than
looking for ways to while away the time. This having "nothing to do" is a most serious and debilitating problem in the later years.

The best way to form your old age is by establishing a pattern in the years of vibrant adulthood. One rock-solid recommendation is to cultivate a real appreciation of Torah study. Then,
when the slow-down time arrives, there is, ready
for the taking, an inexhaustible sea of study with
which to meaningfully fill time.

Too often have I seen patients who vegetate
during illness simply because they have nothing
to do, become bored, and then despair of life. Torah
study links us to our roots, connects us to God, and
gives us a sense of purpose when such infusion is
critical.

But there is more to this preparation than establishing patterns, important as this is. There is
the all-important need to ask what we will do
should some sort of disability, to whatever degree,
invade our lives.

Whatever condition one may be forced to
wrestle with, especially if it is a chronic or possibly
life-threatening situation, the emotional trauma
is quite heavy. It will take the person some time to

adjust to the new situation. For those who, for whatever ridiculous reason, thought that they were immortal and now are told that they have only a certain amount of time left or suddenly realize that they are vulnerable to illness, this may mean a reconsideration of some of the assumptions, however erroneous, that they had made about themselves.

In the process of making this reassessment, such people may be angry at themselves for having been so silly. They may feel a sense of guilt for having been so presumptuous about their longevity that they compromised it. They may blame themselves for having made so many other people dependent upon them. All sorts of emotions go through the mind of a person who has been given so rude a jolt. As difficult as it is to wrestle with these new and painful realities at any time, it is so much easier to do this wrestling in advance.

It helps for people to know that there is no immortality, and that everyone will have to deal with a pack of woes and sorrows in one's lifetime. They may be able to head off or delay some of this with a healthful lifestyle, but inevitably illness catches up to everyone. It is understandable that we should want to push this out of our minds, but it will not go away. Later on, we may be sorry that we did not adequately anticipate these inevitabilities.

There is an instructive story concerning Rabbi Akiva, who was tortured to death by the Romans. As they were mutilating his flesh with iron combs, Rabbi Akiva was accepting upon himself the rulership of Heaven by reciting the Shema (affirmation of faith).

Rabbi Akiva's disciples asked their leader how he could endure this excruciating pain and still be able to recite the Shema. They obviously did not understand how Rabbi Akiva could transcend this pain, or how he could accept upon himself his faith and commitment to God and God's word. Rabbi Akiva's telling response was that, all his life, he was worried about the statement in the Shema that one must love God with all one's soul (Deuteronomy 6:5), meaning, even if God takes away that soul (*Berakhot* 61b). One must be able to express love of God even in the most extenuating circumstances. Rabbi Akiva was anxious about whether, when he came to such a situation, he would be able to fulfill it. Now that the situation had come, he was grateful for the opportunity to fulfill it.

One message of Rabbi Akiva's story is that the best way to handle suffering is to prepare for it in advance. It was precisely because he had anxieties about the suffering, and had mentally conditioned himself that when it came he would be ready for it, that he was, indeed, ready for it.

It is the same for us. Although our suffering is less excruciating, it is still an unavoidable part of life, certainly if we include the vast talmudic definition of anything that is a disappointment or a deviation from a desired plan (see p. 79). The best way to plan for these contingencies is to work them out in our head before their occurrence.

It is, therefore, useful for people to ask themselves, "What will I do if my investment is a total loss? What will I do if, God forbid, I find out that I have an illness? What will I do if something happens to one of my loved ones?" These questions need not be articulated publicly, but they certainly ought to be contemplated in the privacy of one's own thoughts.

In analyzing the questions, one will realize that health is not something that we should take for granted; that everyone will probably have to face some physical difficulties in life, and also will have to wrestle with this happening to loved ones. There is also no guarantee that one will have a job tomorrow, or that one's financial investments will bear fruit.

The same applies to what one will do in the future when things do not go as planned, or when other painful realities are confronted. Anticipating these possibilities and formulating in one's mind how one will react when they occur is most conducive to acting in an appropriate and responsible manner when these events do transpire. Rabbi Akiva set the tone for this with his prior anticipation of having to go through indescribable pain, and being able to do so because he conditioned himself for it cognitively and spiritually.

11
Wrestling with Illness

It is convenient and less threatening to people to see illness as an accident or as attributable to certain events or actions. Rabbi Yehudah HaHasid, in *The Book of the Pious* (*Sefer Hasidim* 751), states that a person when becoming sick, should not think that the illness was caused by having eaten some damaging food or having imbibed some harmful drink and that this was not God's action. Even if one has been attacked by unsavory people, still a person should attribute the suffering to one's own wrongdoings.

This is not necessarily a contradiction of Maimonides' view regarding illness not happening if you take proper care (see p. 57). There is a difference between what happens in advance and what happens after the fact. In advance, one is obliged to take as much care as possible to prevent illness. After an illness does fall upon the individual, even though it may be directly attributable, medically speaking, to injurious eating habits, nevertheless the person should try not only to cure oneself physically, but also to effect some spiritual improvement.

This point is emphasized by Rabbi Eliezer Papo, in his *Pele Yoetz* (under the category of *teva* [nature], p. 263). There he strongly urges individuals never to dismiss what happens to them as being a mere coincidence or an accident. Rather, they should take the attitude that everything that happens is for a purpose. Therefore, if something occurs that has a negative effect on one's health, material well-being, or sense of dignity (i.e., one was insulted or publicly rebuked), one should not dismiss this as being totally unwarranted or explained away by circumstances.

Instead, the person should take this as a message to do some soul-searching. See where you may have gone wrong, and consider it a possible explanation for the calamity. *Pele Yoetz* strongly urges those in all such adverse circumstances to resolve to correct one particular bad habit, and at the same time to adopt one good habit on a regular basis.

In a previous section, Rabbi Papo deals with the question of insult, the insulter, and the insultee. In this discussion, the delicate balance in the circumstances is clear. There is no countenancing a person insulting anyone. To insult others is a terrible evil, which is unconditionally condemned by the talmudic Sages. One who insults a friend in public forfeits any share in the World-to-Come (*Bava Mezia* 59a).

On the other hand, the individual who has been insulted is obliged to engage in soul-searching, on the assumption that there must have been some reason why the insult was given; i.e., that the person deserved the insult (*Pele Yoetz*, p. 62, under the category of *Bizayon*—shame).

There are two issues here. The leveling of the insult is absolutely wrong, an evil that cannot be countenanced. However, once it has already occurred, the person so insulted must look soberly at his or her own behavior to uncover some explanation for what has transpired. Can these two realities be balanced? As far as *Pele Yoetz* is concerned, yes. There is no problem with this type of delicate balance. We can easily adopt a similar attitude with regard to suffering. Absorbing insult is in itself a form of suffering.

This approach can even help somewhat in confronting the overwhelming problem of understanding the meaning of the Holocaust and other great tragedies that the Jewish people have suffered through. The matter is approached with trepidation, owing to the sensitivity of the issue.

There is an interesting sense of balance regarding the massive tragedies that has its precedent in another cataclysmic event in our history: the destruction of the two Holy Sanctuaries, first by the Babylonians and second by the Romans, immense tragedies as graphically detailed in the Book of Lamentations and the Midrash thereon.

Yes, the tragedy of the first destruction was perpetrated by the Babylonians, and the second destruction was perpetrated by the Romans. There is no exonerating them for what they did, and no excusing them for their actions. The same is true of the subjugation inflicted upon the Israelites by Pharaoh, even though it had been foretold that Israel would endure servitude in a foreign land. These individuals and the people who carried out these atrocities did so out of their own choice, and deserve nothing but wholesale condemnation.

On the other hand, when tragedy befell the Jewish people, the Rabbis instructed the people to say such statements as, "Because of our sins we were exiled from our land." Yes, it was the Babylonians and it was the Romans, but if it happened to us, then we must engage in soul-searching. Since we try to elicit meaning from everything in life, we have an obligation to search ourselves to see what we can do to improve ourselves, to make ourselves deserving of a better fate.

Never, for one moment, does this mean excusing the perpetrators of evil. But there is a dialectic here that separates the dispensing of evil and the experiencing of it. It is a very delicate dialectic, and also very necessary, if we are to grow from these experiences and see within them a message that gives us pause and inspires us to reflect and to improve ourselves.

Concerning individual suffering, *Pele Yoetz* also suggests a prayer that one should recite when adverse circumstances arise. This prayer accepts the suffering as deserved and acknowledges that it is designed to bring the sufferer closer to God. The prayer concludes with a request for God's guidance to go in the way of God and the path of the righteous (p. 263).

> Master of the Universe! I am aware of my shame, my embarrassment, and my disgrace, for I have done much to anger You, and You have justly caused me suffering. Please, God, our God and the God of our ancestors, let our prayer come before You and do not be oblivious to our supplication, be close to our entreaty, for we are not so arrogant or stiff-necked as to maintain that we are righteous and have not sinned. Verily we have sinned and You have been righteous in all that has come upon us, for You have acted in truth and we have acted deficiently. To You, God, is mercifulness, for You recompense an individual according to the deeds, to atone for our sins and to guide us towards serving You. Therefore, please, God, compassionate as a father is compassionate on his children, please have compassion upon us. Help us, God of our salvation, for the sake of the glory of Your name, save us and forgive our sins for Your great name sake. Please guide us correctly through Your good counsel so that we walk in the way of goodness and preserve the path of the righteous. May my mouth's utterances and my heart's meditations find favor before You, God, Who is my rock and my redeemer.

This prayer is penetrating. But there is no beating around the bush, no camouflaging the truth, no avoiding what must be confronted. In wrestling with illness, one invariably winds up wrestling with oneself. This way, even if there will be no physical recovery, there will, at the very least, be spiritual rejuvenation.

Many studies indicate that those who are afflicted with suffering generally sink into a more negative behavioral mode rather than becoming ennobled. This does not negate the human capacity to grow in suffering, but it does magnify the enormity of the challenge, and the necessity of meeting the challenge.

12

Fighting the Illness

Jewish tradition views illness as a physical manifestation with spiritual overtones. There is more to the illness than what can be treated by medicine or by a physician.

Generally speaking, however, when a person becomes ill, the first order of business is to attack the illness, to do all that one can to cure it, and to remove the pain. No matter what may be said about the benefits that accrue from illness, pain, and suffering, we should not seek them out. Judaism does not espouse the idea of self-flagellation, suffering, or denial as values in and of themselves.

There are great individuals who live very meager existences, righteous individuals who deny themselves various pleasures of life, but the prevailing motif in Judaism is to fully enjoy this world. We will have to answer for our failure to enjoy the bounty that God has provided (Jerusalem Talmud,

Kiddushin 4:12). This is because we cannot frown upon the world and still express thanks to God for all that God has put in the world. We are primarily obligated to do our best to stay healthy, and, when ill, to do all we can to restore our health.

Reb Hayyim David of Pietrikov suggests that we should approach illness in the order outlined in the blessing, *Yotzer HaMe'orot* (Creator of light). This blessing refers to God as 1) Creator of *healing*; 2) Awesome in *praise*; and 3) Master of *wonder*. First, one must seek a cure (healing). If that does not help, one should resort to *tehilim* (praise). If the situation gets worse, one should not resign oneself to despair; one should, instead, hope for a miracle from the Master of wonders.

We can and should combine seeking a cure with the recitation of *tehilim* (psalms of praise). The first reflex, however, is toward restoration of health. In this process of restoration, there are some enlightening halakhic guidelines.

Rabbi Yehoshua ben Levi (*Shavuot* 15b) states that one is not allowed to cure oneself through words of Torah (*Shulhan Arukh*, Yoreh De'ah 179:9). As clarified by Rabbi Eliezer Waldenburg (*Ziz Eliezer*, Vol. 17, No. 30), this means that one is not allowed to use the Torah as "medicine" when, in fact, it is pharmaceutical medicine that is necessary to heal the patient. To do so would be suicidal behavior.

One can, in addition to medical intervention, continue to study. But to rely solely on study when medical intervention is necessary is not only folly, but prohibited. Words of Torah and *tehilim* (psalms) should accompany the application of appropriate medical treatment, but they must not replace it.

Concerning the medical treatment itself, with regard to a seriously ill person whose physician states that the cure necessitates swallowing a substance that is prohibited by Torah law, Maimonides explicitly states that one must administer all forms of treatment, even prohibited substances, because it is a time of danger. The only exception to this rule is any cure that involves idolatry, sexual immorality, or the spilling of blood (Maimonides, *Laws of the Foundations of the Torah* 5:6).

In other words, we allow almost nothing to stand in the way of the patient's restoration to good health. Additionally, what should ensue is a serious soul-searching that addresses the spiritual side of the illness.

A fascinating dispute centering around a statement in the Talmud serves to clarify this two-pronged approach—physical cure combined with spiritual renewal.

The talmudic statement concerns the Sages' approval of the burying of the book of medicines by the King Hezekiah (*Pesahim* 56a). The reason Rashi offers for this is that the heart of the sick would not be subdued as the result of an immediate recovery. It was more beneficial for the recovery to take longer, and therefore the book of healing, which was able to effect immediate recovery, was buried. That was why it received the hearty endorsement of the Sages.

Maharal, in *Netzah Yisrael* (Chap. 30), goes even further, opining that the reason the Sages applauded the burial of the Book of Cures was so that people should not rely on nature, but rather should pray to God to save them.

On the other hand, Maimonides, in his *Commentary to the Mishnah* (*Pesahim* 4:9) states that the rabbinic endorsement of King Hezekiah's action was for precisely the opposite reason. It was not that the medicine was too effective; it was that the medicine was quackery and a health hazard (see also Walter Wurzburger, *Ethics of Responsibility: Pluralistic Approaches to Covenantal Ethics*, p. 126).

On the surface, the argument between the two luminaries, Rashi and Maimonides, as to the reason for the rabbinic endorsement of the burial of the book seems to involve two extremes: Rashi sees value in a somewhat extended illness for the spiritual benefits it brings, whereas Maimonides insists that one must intervene immediately to intercept the illness and not be concerned about the spiritual implications.

Rashi's suggestion that the Sages praised the burial of the book of healing because the patient's heart would not be subdued as a result of immediate recovery (*Pesahim* 56a)—that they had no chance to contemplate the meaning of their illness and to repent—may be expressing a notion that has its analogue in certain approaches to medicine.

We are able to mask certain symptoms with medications that do not necessarily cure, but merely alleviate the symptoms. If a person feels ill, there is a full range of possible factors that may have generated this condition. The real cure is not in giving medication to mask the symptoms, but rather in understanding the genesis of the illness and treating the illness at its core. This approach is a primary feature of homeopathic practice, for example. Homeopathy is a well-accepted medical approach fully covered by government health insurance in many European countries.

Rashi may be suggesting that since illness is related to certain deficiencies, there are reasons for the occurrence of the illness, including the strong possibility that it is due to things the person has done wrong. It would then be advantageous for the patient to try to figure out the reasons for this visitation of illness, to get to the root of it and thereby eradicate it.

Let us illustrate this with an example. Consider someone who has a headache. That person can take a pill that will remove the pain associated with the headache, but this does not necessarily mean that the person is rid of the problem. The potential causes of the headache are numerous, including some serious possibilities. Continual masking of this symptom will delay the actual uncovering of the root cause of the headache—clearly not good medicine. We understand this on a purely medical level.

But there is also a spiritual level to illness. Rashi is suggesting that we must endeavor to understand the illness, and not try to instantaneously make believe that it is not there. Pretense through symptom removal is less than beneficial for the patient.

This does not mean that we seek illness, or that we do not do our utmost to eliminate the illness. It means only that we should not, in our haste to remove the illness, forget about searching out why the illness occurred in the first place. Soul-searching is good medicine—good biological medicine and good spiritual medicine.

This explanation minimizes, to some degree, what at first glance seems to be a major dispute between Rashi and Maimonides. Both, it turns out, agree that the Book of Healing contained bad medicine that, if implemented, was not conducive to ultimate cure. Since it failed to address the entire scope of a medical problem, it was deemed by Maimonides to be quackery, an assessment that Rashi endorsed, albeit from a different perspective.

If we take the attitude that suffering is potentially a positive component of human life, and that instant symptom removal is not ideal medical practice, does this in any way impact on our attitude towards pain and suffering? Should we, when faced with a pain situation, actually endure the pain rather than try to alleviate it? Is there any room for a theological suggestion to actually avoid the pills that will eliminate the pain?

These ideas are as preposterous as the suggestion that because our life destiny is in God's hands, we have no obligation to guard our lives carefully. We know that this is not the case from the host of regulations that fall under the rubric of the responsibility to care for life. Why not make the argument that since it is all in God's hands, and only God determines how long we are going to live, then it makes no difference whether or not we preserve our health?

The answer is that it *does* make a difference. God has specifically obliged each one of us to take care of the life that has been given to us, and that we are entrusted with maintaining it. It is not a one-sided relationship in which everything is God's responsibility; it is a partnership. It is a partnership in which God specifically tells us, God's designated partners: If you show that you care about your own life, then I will also care. But if you do not take care of your life, then you have no right to expect that I will take care of that life.

So, the individual who smokes three packs of cigarettes a day, finds out that he has lung cancer, and then says, "Why did God do this to me?" is out of bounds. Knowing what we know about tobacco and cancer, we could say that this is the equivalent of jumping off a bridge and expecting to survive the fall. Pertinent to this is Maimonides' observation that self-inflicted suffering is the most frequent cause of human grief (*The Guide of the Perplexed* 3:12).

Because we are mortal and frail, and far from perfect, it is quite likely that we will do things in life that will negatively affect our health. Illness, therefore, is not abnormal; illness is normal. We are all likely to experience illness of one form or another in our lifetime. Unquestionably, as previously mentioned, the first impulse and the most powerful reaction that we must implement is to fight it; to fight it with all our strength, and to attempt to overcome the illness.

It makes no difference whether we are talking about the common cold, flu, severe stomachaches, and headaches, or more pernicious and life-threatening illnesses such as cancer, heart disease, or other cardiovascular disorders. There are, of course, the chronic diseases, the ones that can be with us for a protracted period, including arthritis, Parkinson's disease, and colitis. These, too, demand a vigorous response

It is easier said than done, but truly it is helpful to be able to put on a positive face despite the illness. The best of us has low points when wrestling with disease; but low points either can be the defining points or they can just be the blips, the exceptions to the general rule. The rabbinic observation, "Whoever rejoices in the suffering that befalls them brings salvation to the world" (*Taanit* 8a), is an instructive model for how we should approach illness. The implication of this model is that we should try to maintain our presumably happy demeanor even in the face of illness.

The cultivation of a positive attitude to suffering should begin long before the suffering situation presents itself. And aside from confronting the inevitability of suffering and contemplating how it will be handled, we can work on the general attitudinal approach to life.

A good teacher of this attitudinal approach is the talmudic sage Shmuel. Shmuel (*Berakhot* 55b), when he had a bad dream, simply uttered the words, "And dreams speak falsehood." These words are from a verse in Zekharyah 10:2. However, when Shmuel had a good dream, he would turn around these same words and say, "Do dreams really speak falsehood? Does it not state, "In a dream I will speak to him?" (Numbers 12:6).

In other words, when the dream was a good one, Shmuel would readily welcome it, but when it was a bad one, he would reject it. This speaks quite convincingly about the human capacity to control the messages that are filtering into the system; to throw away those that are undesirable and to accept those that are desirable. How we interpret what happens to us is, therefore, quite an important matter, a matter that is in our hands.

Through a simple exercise regarding dreams, we can convince ourselves of our ability to control our thoughts and generate the confidence that we can wrestle with more difficult challenges down the road, when maintaining a happy demeanor is essential during the throes of illness and suffering.

Another important attitude to cultivate is to be accepting of others. The general pattern among most people is that they are very demanding of others, but very undemanding of themselves. They find fault in others and blame them, while at the same time they refuse to acknowledge that they, too, have faults or are deserving of blame.

Insult is one area wherein this pattern is particularly pronounced. Most people are quite sensitive to the insults hurled at them, but refuse to believe that they have insulted others, even if they are told that they have been insulting. The ideal is to be careful with the dignity and honor of others, and not so meticulous concerning oneself (*Shabbat* 88b; *Yoma* 23a).

This attitude is reflected in the aforementioned statement of Rabbi Ada, son of Ahavah—also attributed to Rabbi Zayra—that links his longevity to, among other things, not having been demanding of respect within the household (*Taanit* 20b; *Megillah* 28a).

Interestingly, included in the cluster of laudable character traits (*Shabbat* 88b; *Yoma* 23a) regarding accepting insult but not dispensing it, is the attribute of "being happy in affliction." There is a logical connection between being able to accept insult and being able to accept suffering. Insult is, after all, a form of suffering (see Rashi for *Shabbat* 88b, on *osin ma'ahavat haMakom usmayhim b'yisurim*).

These helpful attitudes, emphasizing the good and accepting the untoward, do more than improve one's ability to overcome the illness. Such attitudes also make life easier for everyone around the ill person. It is normally the case that people will feel helpless if they have to contend with a cranky, complaining, nagging patient.

Nurses in hospitals will readily testify that they not only find it much easier to treat happy and cooperative patients, but they are generally more likely to be helpful to such individuals than they are to those who are complainers. It is natural for human beings to behave this way—to be comfortable with those whose behavior puts them at ease, and to withdraw from those whose behavior makes them feel ill at ease.

The rabbinic adage praising the person who maintains a happy posture even in the midst of suffering therefore speaks directly not only to the spiritual side, but to the purely practical side of life, especially when illness must be confronted with the help of others.

13

Inspirational Fighters

Attitude to suffering is more than an intangible; it has a direct impact on the ability of those who are suffering to endure the pain, and to survive. The following study in contrast, in the unfolding lives of Sue Rodriguez and Sam Filer, illustrates this point quite emphatically.

A number of years ago, Canada was caught up in the haunting plight of Sue Rodriguez, a relatively young woman who had been diagnosed with amyotrophic lateral sclerosis (ALS), otherwise known as Lou Gehrig's disease. She did not want to suffer the agonies of ALS, and had petitioned the Court for the legal right to have herself gently put away by doctor-assisted suicide.

The Supreme Court, in a very close decision, denied her request, but Sue Rodriguez had the last word. She arranged for a doctor to terminate her life, and this was done in the utmost secrecy. To this day, no one knows the name of the doctor who actually performed this "humanitarian" act.

Contrast the case of Sue Rodriguez with that of Justice Sam Filer, a judge in the Ontario Court, General Division. As reported in the December 7, 1995 issue of the *Canadian Jewish News* (p. 21), Filer is a man who, believe it or not, counts his blessings. He is completely paralyzed, except for a muscle in his cheek and some limited eye movement, as a result of ALS; yet he is able to concentrate on what he has in life, rather than on what he has lost.

Filer's remarkable courage has earned him the Clarke Institute of Psychiatry Foundation's Courage to Come Back Award and the Bronfman Medal of the Canadian Jewish Congress. Furthermore, the Canadian Jewish Congress has established the Sam N. Filer Award, which is given to people who demonstrate exemplary service to the Jewish community.

Filer was diagnosed with ALS in 1987, and within a year he was using a wheelchair. He almost died from lung failure in 1989, and his wife Toni, against the doctors' recommendations, insisted that he be surgically connected to a respirator so that he could continue to live. Filer communicates by way of Morse-code impulses sent through a mioelectric conductor to his cheek. The impulses are sent to a computer, voice synthesizer, and printer.

Filer is quoted as saying, "I admit that there was a time when I used to wake up each morning wondering what else I was going to be unable to do, but through Toni's infinite patience, guidance and wisdom, and the love of my four children, I began to focus on those abilities which I still retained, rather than mourn those which I lost."

It is mind-boggling to realize that Filer works three days a week at home and spends two days a week in his judicial chambers. Civil liberties, human rights, social justice, and Jewish community issues all are vital parts of his life.

In Filer's words, "It is important to me to continue working and to be involved in the community. I share the same needs as everyone else—to be a productive, contributing member of society and to my chosen profession. I enjoy being in the company of colleagues and friends who I respect and who regard me in terms of what I can do, not what I can't." Filer goes to the theater, entertains friends, and watches his daughter play baseball.

Filer's thoughts about what he has learned since contracting ALS are instructive in their eloquence. He says:

> Above all, love, friendship, faith in God, and a feeling of self-worth, no matter how it's derived, are powerful elixirs, particularly when there is no medical treatment available. A diagnosis of ALS need not be accompanied by an automatic death sentence. Inexperienced, able-bodied people, whether doctors or not, are not necessarily the best people to determine whether a quadriplegic who cannot speak, eat or breathe without mechanical assistance, can enjoy a meaningful quality of life. I enjoy doing many things with my family and friends. Recognizing my mind–body connection, I don't think of myself as suffering

from, a victim of, or dying from ALS. In truth,
I'm living as best as I can with ALS.

These are stirring words from a man who is in
the midst of a terribly debilitating disease that has
had a horrible effect on his elementary functionality, but who has managed to overcome because
he has the right attitude, the right family support,
and, yes, the right faith. What a difference between
Sue Rodriguez, whose ALS was not nearly as advanced as Sam Filer's and who chose to terminate
her life, and the courageous example of Sam Filer,
who said yes to life unconditionally and without
reservation.

This difference is rooted in divergent attitudes
to life and to suffering. However, this is not intended to castigate Rodriguez. As will become evident in the discussion on suicide (see Chapter 28),
it is not the Jewish way to condemn individuals
after the suicide has taken place. We do not know
the suffering or the mental torment that Rodriguez
endured. At the same time, it is possible—and
proper—to laud Sam Filer's way as being most consistent with Judaic life-affirming values.

Attitude to suffering goes beyond maintaining a happy face. It encompasses the capacity to
affirm life in spite of the difficulty in actualizing
such affirmation. This capacity was uniquely
achieved by a heroic young woman who con-
tracted breast cancer.

This young woman was full of vigor, had done
magnificent things within the community, and at

the same time was the mother of five lovely children and wife of a very appreciative husband. She had everything to live for. The news that she had cancer came as a crushing piece of news to her, and was a profound shock to the entire community. But she fought back, had surgery, and everything was fine. So everyone thought—until it became clear that the cancer had spread.

The young woman's chances of survival were quite minimal. But she fought with every ounce of strength that she had to overcome this pernicious disease. On what was to be one of the last days of her life, when she was attached to a morphine pump and was seemingly unable to get around, I went to visit her in the hospital. But she was not in her room. I went to the nurses' station to ask where she was, and they told me that she had gone out for lunch. I looked quizzically at the nurses, insisting that she was in no shape to go out, especially since she was hooked to a morphine pump. The nurses stood firm, insisting that friends had come, and that she had gone out—out of the hospital, that is—for lunch with them.

I went away totally perplexed, and returned the next day to visit this extraordinary woman. This time, I found her in her room, and it was clear that she was failing rapidly and was not going to last more than another day or two.

She did have enough strength to talk, however. I asked her whether she had been out to lunch the day before, and she acknowledged that, yes, she had gone out with her friends. I asked her how she could do it, being that she was in such a state, and that this effort entailed so much difficulty. Her response was inspirational beyond words.

She told me that when she realized that she was fighting an uphill battle and that there was a good chance she would not make it, she resolved that she was not going to die every day of the rest of her life, that she was not going to die her living; instead, she was going to live her dying. What she desired was to live every day that she had in the best possible fashion. She was going to try to squeeze as much out of life as she could.

I knew, as I was hearing these words, that not only was this an extraordinary response, but it was a response totally consistent with Jewish ideals. The idea that even when we know that we are terminally ill, we should fight back and squeeze out of life as much as we can, is the best way to affirm life—to affirm our love of life and our love of God even in the worst of circumstances (i.e., even though God takes away your life—*Berakhot* 61b).

In effect, it shows that our commitment to life is unconditional, and prevails under all conditions. Certainly, for this young woman, those conditions were excruciating pain, the terrible anguish of knowing that death was around the corner, and the knowledge that her beloved husband and children would soon be bereft of their wife and mother. Still, with all this physical and emotional pain, to be able to muster up the courage, the vigor, and the determination to manifest a sense of life-affirmation under these excruciating conditions was truly extraordinary.

This was a subconscious expression of saintliness, although the young woman would have rejected any such claim. Nevertheless, years after her passing, I still vividly recall this as an outstanding example of what it is to affirm life up to the very last moment. It is a model of transcending, to whatever extent possible, the adverse circumstances with which we are confronted at some point in our lives, and making the most of whatever we have.

Perhaps the most inspiring reaction to illness involves Jay Feinberg and his family. In his early twenties, Jay was diagnosed with chronic myelogenous leukemia. At the time, he had just graduated with high honors and had gone to work as a foreign-exchange analyst at the Federal Reserve Bank.

To save his life, Jay needed a bone-marrow transplant from a suitable donor. His was a difficult type to match, however, and the search went beyond the three-year window following diagnosis, beyond which time the chances for survival are bleak. In the end, a donor was found—not a perfect match, but good enough for a successful graft. The donor was the last person tested in the last blood drive of a search that went on for four years!

That Jay was able to persevere until a suitable match was found is a story in itself. But the real inspiration is the dedication of Jay and his parents, Jacob and Arlene Feinberg. In the midst of their desperate search for a donor for their son, Arlene and Jacob made it clear that no matter what the outcome, they would dedicate their lives to finding matching donors for those needing bone-marrow transplants.

When Jay was in the hospital for the long, arduous transplant procedure, Arlene vigilantly watched him, and simultaneously maintained contact with other transplant recipients who had found matching donors from drives that had been run for Jay. An organization called Friends of Jay had been established, and this organization, headed by the Feinbergs, continues in the *shadkhan* (matchmaking) business, trying to find compatible bone-marrow donors for those in need. More than sixty thousand people have been screened through Friends of Jay alone, matching the entire number of people that have been screened in Canada!

The Feinbergs have transformed a challenge to life into a life's challenge to help as many people as possible. Instead of complaining about their fate, they have transformed crisis into opportunity. Their lives have changed dramatically, and their priorities have shifted focus almost exclusively to saving lives.

The Feinbergs did not seek the suffering, but when the illness and anguish overcame them, they refused to surrender. They changed their lives, and that change, they would argue, was undoubtedly for the better—for a life suffused with meaning and purpose.

14

Accepting Mortality

One of the most difficult issues, if not the most difficult to handle when confronting suffering is the guilt factor. Telling a person who is contending with painful affliction that this condition is due to their wrongdoing adds insult to injury. It is counterproductive for anyone to suggest such a thing to a suffering person. On the other hand, it is a well-accepted tenet of Judaism that suffering is usually related to human failing. If such is the case, how can the message be transmitted?

Essentially, the message should not be transmitted at all. The message is one that we all should integrate into our psyches long before the affliction presents itself. We should accept our mortality long before mortality makes its first inroads into our physical equilibrium.

Accepting mortality means more than realizing that we will not live forever; it is to realize that we are mortal in space as well as in time, that we are psychically mortal and thus prone to error, sin, and failing. We should not be ashamed of this, since we all share the same tendencies. "For there is no righteous individual on earth who does good and will not sin" (Ecclesiastes 7:20). No one is perfect. To pretend that we are perfect is the worst of all human character failings, for it means that we are always right, can do no wrong, and do not need the advice and illumination of parents and teachers. This is arrogance of the worst sort, and is bound to lead to a host of personal and relational difficulties.

Therefore, accepting that suffering is due to our human failing is nothing more than the acknowledgment of fundamental human reality. The words of the outstanding talmudic expositor known as Meiri are quite striking in this context.

Meiri says that there is no person who has not sinned even lightly or without even sensing that one has done so, whether in word, in thought, or in failing to act. Failing to be involved in Torah can cause suffering. This failure may manifest itself in failing to protest an issue when it was within one's power to do so; it also may manifest in a person's not attaining personal completeness to the point where it is impossible to find any iniquity or sin within the person.

Because of the lightness of the person's sin, that person will receive only a light punishment, which is so subtle that the person will not sense that it is a reaction to the person's having done wrong. Because of the failure to sense this, the person will not be inspired to repent, but will continue in the previously lightly embraced ways.

It is of the mercies of God's love that the punishment is increased to the point where the person sees the connection between the sin and the behavior, senses the light sins, and repents from them. A person is never punished for no reason, Meiri adduces all this from the fact that the Sages have brought as a proof for this the verse: "It is the one that God loves that God rebukes" (Proverbs 3:12). This language of rebuke is not employed merely with someone who had behaved in a way that would deserve rebuke in order to remove a habit or character trait (Shever Gaon, first essay, Chap. 4, *Hibur HaTeshuvah L'Rabbenu Menahem ben R' Shelomoh HaMeiri*, Talpiyot, New York: Yeshiva University, 1950).

This same approach is developed in Rabbi Yehudah HaLevi's *Kuzari* (essay 2, no. 58). He speaks about plagues visited on houses and garments as related to light breaches, and more severe breaches manifesting on the body in varying degrees of intensity, related to the seriousness of the trespass. It was the task of the *kohen* (spiritual leader in the Holy Sanctuary) to discern which visitation was actually a castigation from Above.

It is not easy to accept that suffering is a sign of caring, of God's concern about who we are and how we are. But that, according to Jewish tradition, is the fact.

What should a person do who has been told, "You have only a limited time to live"? The old Jewish joke is that the first thing to do is to go for a second opinion. That is not merely a joke; it is also sound advice. But what if the second opinion is exactly the same as the first opinion? Then what?

In such circumstances, it is important to put one's house in order and to establish what our priorities are in life. For some people, it may mean enjoying some of the things that they never had time to enjoy. But this is all transitory pleasure that does not have long-lasting meaning. The best approach in such situations is to think along the lines of ultimate values. This is a sound approach in all circumstances, but it is particularly appropriate when the ultimate is slowly but surely coming into focus.

In thinking about what will happen after one is gone, it is best to engage in introspection, to see where and how one can improve oneself; to assess those things in life that one could have done better; those things in life that one has not done at all; and to determine where one can make theoretical, mental, and even practical improvements along those themes.

"Repent one day before your death," advises the Talmud (*Shabbat* 153a). Since we do not know when that will be, we should engage in repentance and self-improvement every day (ibid.). We tend to avoid this meaningful exercise, but we certainly should not continue to avoid it after we have been given an indication of our own mortality.

If, for example, one had opportunities for charitable work when one was well but did not take advantage of them, the opportunity to be philanthropic, if it is still available, should now be embraced with eagerness. To leave a legacy is one of the most important activities a human being can be involved with.

If personal relationships that are grounded in love have not been as intense as they should be, or even in their intensity leave room for further elaboration and connectedness, this, too, should be worked on. To further strengthen the relationship with one's spouse or one's child is most worthwhile.

How often have I seen children whose melancholy after their parents have died is due to the fact that their parents never told them how they truly felt about them. Conversely, how spiritually uplifting and helpful it is toward long-range recovery from tragedy for parents to explicitly tell their children how much they love them, appreciate them, care for them, and admire them. They may be only words, but they are heartfelt and uplifting words that make the difference between depression and recovery for the grieving loved ones left behind.

Similarly, in the deepening of a relationship between spouses, this approach has tremendous benefit for the surviving spouse. True, intense love makes the tragedy of the passing much more painful. Love and suffering go hand-in-hand. In the long run, however, the pleasant memories that are left behind more than amply compensate for this.

One heroic woman, for whom I always had tremendous admiration because she was so full of energy and genuinely gushing with joy and a genuine desire to help others, suddenly was struck with a cancer that proved to be fatal. In the last days of her life, blessed as she was with a devoted and loving husband, she made it clear to him that after she died, she wanted him to remarry, so that he could find happiness again and their children would have someone to take care of them with the devotion of a mother.

How beautiful a legacy it is for a husband to be given such a wish from his dying and beloved spouse. Most people in such situations are hesitant about remarrying, thinking—wrongly—that this would be disloyal to their first spouse. They are, therefore, overloaded with unnecessary guilt at even contemplating such a thought.

How wonderful it is when the dying spouse actually advocates remarriage. In this way, the surviving partner, in remarrying, actually fulfills the wishes of the beloved departed mate. There is no guilt; on the contrary, there is a feeling that you are doing something to perpetuate the memory of the deceased by fulfilling the deceased's wishes.

V

ISSUES IN SUFFERING

15
Why Suffer?

The question "Why suffer?" is both a philosophical-theological query and a practical lament. The person confronting a painful illness may question the worthwhileness of the struggle to overcome the illness, especially if the odds of succeeding are not great.

The issue of why we should suffer and its link to doctor-assisted suicide presently occupies center stage in North America. In the United States, Dr. Jack Kevorkian, sometimes ingloriously called "Dr. Death," has gained fame and notoriety by means of his intervening to snuff out the lives of people who desired to be relieved of their suffering. In his campaign to legalize doctor-assisted suicide, Dr. Kevorkian has articulated an approach to medicine that may be called Kevorkianism. This is a gut-wrenching issue: "Why suffer; why live; why not suicide?"

Jewish tradition does not grant the physician carte blanche in the healing process. The physician has permission to heal—nothing more.

On the biblical statement alluding to the healing process in duplicate language—i.e., ". . . and heal, the doctor shall heal" (Exodus 21:20)—the Talmud states that this thereby conveys God's authorization for physicians to heal (*Bava Kama* 85a). Presumably, without this authorization, medical intervention would be considered problematic. In retrospect, it is difficult to imagine that God would have enjoined the practice of medicine, especially in light of the multitude of medically sensitive regulations in the Torah.

The message in this permission-granting most likely is that all doctors must realize that their healing mandate comes from God. That mandate is to heal, not to kill. A physician who cannot heal, for whatever reason, including when the illness has advanced far beyond healing, has no right to take life, any more than any person has the right to take life.

The biblical obligation to restore what someone has lost (Deuteronomy 22:2) is the basis for the obligation to restore one's health (*Sanhedrin* 73a). Maimonides, in his Commentary on the Mishnah (*Nedarim* 38b), quotes this verse about restoring what was lost—namely, health—as the basis for the physician's obligation to heal. First, the physician is granted permission. Then, permission having been granted, the doctor has the obligation to engage in the "healing" process, to restore health.

Suicide is forbidden, according to Jewish law. No one has the right to commit suicide; and, by definition, no one has the right to assist others in a forbidden activity such as suicide. The doctor who so "assists" not only contravenes fundamental Jewish law, but also renounces the very mandate that allows for the practice of medicine in the first place. That is the limited mandate to heal—not a mandate to kill, or to help in the killing.

Jewish law on Kevorkianism is quite straightforward, with no room for equivocation. Kevorkianism is rejected, which comes as little surprise.

The sympathies of the public, however, seem to be on Kevorkian's side. The public at large is becoming more accepting of the "Hemlock society" approach to suffering. In a world devoid of ultimate meaning, why suffer? To that question there is no answer. But to the hypothesis that life, and the suffering it brings, has no meaning, there is an eloquent Judaic retort, a retort that precludes the question. It is, unfortunately, a retort that escapes the proponents of Kevorkianism.

Within the Judaic context, it is important to directly address the philosophical–theological aspect of the question why one should suffer. If this is not done, then chances are greater that what presently may only be a practical lament about suffering will become a strategy of refusal to fight the illness. It is, therefore, essential to try to answer this question on a theoretical level, but to avoid the glib explanations offered to Job by his friends, so that the practical approach does not become one of resignation, or even possibly suicide, assisted or otherwise.

Rav Huna, in *Midrash Rabbah* (Genesis 1:31), explains that the words "and behold, it was very good," apply to the dispensation of suffering. The Midrash asks: Can, then, suffering actually be very good? To which the Midrash responds: It is, in fact, so because through suffering humankind attains the life of the future world.

Rabbi Eliezer Papo, in his *Pele Yo'etz* (p. 290), urges the individual to accept all suffering with joy, happiness, and goodness of heart. The person should say about any suffering that this, too, is for the good, and whatever God does is for the good. Indeed that is the case, because what seems to be bad in the eyes of the human being, God thought of for the good. The problem is that, at times, these reasons are in the realm of the hidden that is known only to God, but at other times they will eventually become known to us. But at all times we can give meaning and purpose to the circumstance of suffering.

Rabbi Yohanan observed that Israel is compared to an olive. Just as oil is extractable from the olive only upon the olive's being crushed, so, too, does Israel return to the good only by affliction. The point here is that affliction is not intended as a punishment, but as a corrective (*Menahot* 53b). It is for the ultimate good, however undesirable it may be at the moment.

There is a fascinating story in the Talmud (*Berakhot* 5b) about Rabbi Yohanan, who felt weak and faint. Rabbi Hanina went to visit him, and asked: "Is the suffering precious to you?" Rabbi Yohanan responded honestly: "Not the suffering and not its rewards." Rabbi Hanina then said: "Give me your hand." Rabbi Yohanan extended his hand, and Rabbi Hanina raised him up. In fact, he extricated him from the suffering.

The nature of Rabbi Yohanan's suffering is not clear. It is possible that it was a general malaise not disassociated from depression, which weakened him and made it difficult for him to go out, and that Rabbi Hanina helped him out of his depression.

Maharal speaks about the fact that even with regard to afflictions emanating from God's love, it is not in our capacity to understand this. There are righteous people who do not desire these afflictions, as illustrated in the famous story of the talmudist Rabbi Yohanan (*Berakhot* 5b), who wanted neither the suffering nor its rewards.

From this it is obvious that these afflictions are difficult for even the righteous to endure, even if they were caused to occur out of love and to increase their meritoriousness. It is stated that it is not in our capacity to appreciate the tranquility of the wicked or even the affliction of the righteous (Maharal, *Derekh Hayyim* 4:16).

The further implication of the talmudic story involving Rabbi Yohanan is that suffering has value only if we value it. If we do not desire the suffering, then the suffering can be destructive rather than constructive.

But we do not always have the power to simply eliminate the cause of the suffering. Inoperable cancer, chronic arthritis, or kidney failure may be too difficult to eliminate. We may be able to anesthetize the physical pain, but the mental torment of someone who is aware that a pernicious disease is eating away at the body cannot be assuaged by any medicine.

The person can be put out of commission—in a sense, almost made to be spiritually dead—with powerful painkillers, but that certainly does not solve the problem of suffering; it merely evades it. We may have alleviated the cause, but not the reason for, the anguish.

We can fight the illness, and also not allow the pain and discomfort to compromise our resolve and our affirmative approach to life. But that is not a simple task. It helps to keep matters in focus by fully appreciating that the Godly intent in the suffering is for the good.

The statement by Rabbi Yehoshua, the son of Levi, that whoever rejoices in their suffering brings salvation to the world (*Taanit* 8a) expresses the most exalted manner of confronting suffering.

The idea inherent in this is that we all suffer, and that if one can maintain a happy face and go through life in spite of the suffering, this is salvational. It inspires others to go forward and to endure, rather than to be swallowed up and rendered useless by the suffering. Inspiring others to continue in life is, by definition, salvational.

16

Finding a
Meaning in Suffering

The issue of how to wrestle with suffering obviously goes beyond theory. It is an issue that touches the very core of existence, and the roots of meaningful survival. One of the three types of people of whom the Sages said that their life is not a life, is one whose affliction rules one's body (*Betzah* 32b).

It is important to note that the Talmud does not speak about someone who is undergoing suffering; rather, it refers to someone whose suffering rules over him or her. In other words, if life has reached the point wherein the suffering is so intense that there is no functionality, this type of situation is untenable.

Different people have different tolerance levels for pain. However, it is possible to experience and to persevere through excruciating pain if one is able to transcend the pain. In many instances, just the fact that there is a meaning attributed to the pain and to the suffering, or a meaning beyond this—i.e., even a meaning associated with *olam haba*, the World-to-Come—can be a significant help in transcending the physical complications.

Rabbi Ami (*Shabbat* 55a) states that there is no death without sin, and no affliction without iniquity. This is a supreme categorical statement. Rabbi Shimon ben Elazar disputes this, maintaining that there can be death without sin, and affliction without iniquity. The Talmud confirms this view, citing examples of people who died even though they had not sinned. Tosafot (*Shabbat* 55b, starting with the words *u'shma mi'nah*) notes that the refutation of Rabbi Ami in the Talmud concerned only the death part, not the affliction part. Nevertheless, the Talmud sees suffering and death as a package. If there can be death without sin, then there can be suffering without iniquity.

The oft-quoted verse, "For there is no righteous individual on earth who does good and will not sin" (Ecclesiastes 7:20), seemingly indicates that we all sin, and that therefore there could be no death without sin, since there is no life without sin. Tosafot (*Shabbat* 55b, beginning *Arba'ah maytu*) remarks that this verse refers to most people. There are rare exceptions—people who never sin; and since the exceptions also die, the causal link between death and sinfulness is detached. There can be death without sin, but in most instances, there is sin and there is death that is related to sin.

Similarly, there is suffering without iniquity, but in most cases where there is suffering, it is related to iniquity. Perhaps basic to the idea of suffering related to iniquity is the proposition that we look upon God not as generous and overlooking evil, but rather as One Who metes out justice according to deservedness.

In the end, what God does is purely God's business. But from a moral and ethical perspective, were we to approach our responsibility with a laxity that comes from the belief—or the likelihood—that God will be understanding and forgiving, then we would likely capitulate on our values in a very dangerous way. It is therefore important for us to work with the uncompromising proposition that we get what we deserve and we will not get what we do not deserve.

Thus, Rabbi Hanina said: "If one says that the Holy One, blessed is God, is lax in the execution of justice, that one's life shall be unruly, for it is stated (Deuteronomy 32:4)—'The Rock, God's work is perfect, for all God's ways are judgment'" (*Bava Kama* 50a).

God is not lax, and God's agenda in dispensing affliction is not necessarily to be construed as punishment. In the view of the *Zohar*, affliction may be intended as enlightenment.

> When God desires the soul of the individual, to enlighten it, God afflicts the body so that the soul should gain supremacy, because as long as the soul and the body are equal, the soul cannot dominate, but when the body is broken, the soul reigns supreme (*Zohar*, Toldot 90, in *Sefer HaZohar al Hamishah Humshay Torah* [10 vols.], London: 1970).

The message of the *Zohar* is that rather than being angry at God for our affliction, we should instead be grateful and thankful. Granted, this is not the way people usually react to suffering, but that is related to the failure to apprehend why God has imposed the suffering. It is in this regard that Rabbi Elazar the son of Yaakov states that one should be grateful to God in the time that afflictions come upon the person. Why? Because the afflictions draw the person closer to God (*Midrash Tanhuma*, Ki Teze 2). But that closeness will evolve only if the afflicted person appreciates the design of God as being a constructive design.

Further along this theme, Rabbi Yonatan states that affliction is precious because a covenant was established concerning affliction. Rabbi Shimon son of Yohai asserts that affliction is precious because three lovely gifts were given to Israel through affliction: 1) the Torah; 2) the land of Israel; and 3) *olam haba* (the World-to-Come). In other words, we attain eternity only through affliction (*Mekhilta*, Yitro Sec. 10; also *Berakhot* 5a).

Why are these indispensable gifts associated with prior affliction? Unlike typical gifts, which are dropped into one's hand, these three are gifts there for us to take. We must work hard for them, and must even suffer to attain them. This readiness indicates that we are aware of how important these three ingredients are in our life, so important that we will endure whatever is thrown our way to attain them. In other words, we receive these gifts because we work for them. They reflect our achievement.

A person's suffering may be intended for the purpose of achieving enlightenment, but it may also be related to our wrongdoing. How are we to know what is behind the suffering? We can discern what is behind the suffering only if we go about the process of self-investigation honestly, willing to admit to our failings and ready to correct them.

The actual process is formulated in the Talmud: If a person sees affliction coming, that person should investigate one's deeds, and see if there is any causal connection between the misbehavior and the affliction being endured. If after investigation the person can find nothing to explain the suffering, the affliction should be attributed to the failure to use available moments to study God's Torah. If even this is not a legitimate explanation, then it is clear that these are afflictions of love.

Rashi takes this to mean that these afflictions are unrelated to any sinfulness, and are intended to ensure that one's deservedness in this world exceeds one's merits. Consistent with this, Rava in the name of Rav Sehorah in the name of Rav Huna asserts that whomever God strongly desires, God will crush in affliction. This is on the proviso that the person accepts the afflictions with love, for otherwise it would be counterproductive.

The Talmud goes on to present two views of what is considered an affliction of love. One view is that it is only an affliction of love if it does not entail the inability to study Torah; the other view is that it is only an affliction of love if it does not entail the inability to pray. Ostensibly, the pur-

pose of the suffering is to bring one closer to God;
if it achieves just the opposite, it cannot be considered an affliction of love. This position is articulated quite clearly by the Maharal (see pp. 174–75).

However, the Talmud's final view is that even
these afflictions may actually be afflictions of love.
Apparently, if one cannot pray or study Torah, this
does not necessarily mean that the person is es-
tranged from God or cannot become closer to God
(*Berakhot* 5a).

Parenthetically, all of this places a different
perspective on the pain in childbirth, which is normally looked upon as a curse. But in the same way
that suffering—which one normally does not seek
out—is seen from a different and constructive
perspective, so must we reinvestigate the notion
that pain in childbirth is intended for punitive
purposes.

Yes, this pain was in reaction to an episode
involving the noncompliance of Eve and Adam
with a divine directive (Genesis 2:16). But this does
not necessarily lead to the conclusion that what
God instituted afterwards is a curse. After all, there
is the larger question of why future generations
should have to suffer because of what was perpetrated by Adam and Eve. Rabbi Samson Raphael
Hirsch suggests that this is not necessarily a punishment, but a corrective reaction. Because life was
too easy, and the human being exerted no sweat
and toil in order to glean from the world, there
was, therefore, a lack of appreciation of all the
bounty that was bestowed upon humankind.

However, because of the renunciation and pain involved in the childbirth process, a closeness develops between the mother and the child. The child's coming into this world is linked directly to the alleviation of the excruciating labor pains. The intense pain persists up to the point of fulfillment, but the fulfillment comes as an alleviation of the pain, and signals the prospect of greater fulfillment in the future. Additionally, the birth takes place after hard work, and is therefore more likely to be appreciated.

Concerning the need to work as a result of the breach in the Garden of Eden, the Torah states that "for your sake is the ground restrained" (Genesis 3:7). The change that takes place may seem to be a change for the worse, but, in fact, it is a change "for your sake." It is for our benefit. It is how we connect with the world, and the betterment of the world is connected to our efforts (see further, Hirsch's commentary on this verse).

Windfalls may appear to be blessings, but in the end they are just the opposite. Prosperity that simply falls into our hands is not nearly as appreciated and nurtured as prosperity that comes from earning it and contributing to a better world. This meaningful prosperity involves more sweat and toil, but it is our sweat, our achievement, and therefore our potential spiritual enlightenment.

But we must maintain the proper perspective in all this. We dare not run after suffering, or to consider suffering to be a value in and of itself. Walter Wurzburger makes the compelling point

that the value that can be extracted from suffering
does not make suffering an intrinsic value. Instead,
the value of suffering is a means to an end; suffering is not an end in itself (*Ethics of Responsibility*, pp.
53–55).

Suffering and the meaning attached to it are
key elements not only on a personal level. The
community of Israel was forged in suffering, a suffering that was preordained. Abraham was told by
God that his descendants will be strangers in a land
that is not theirs, and they will be enslaved and
afflicted for a protracted length of time (Genesis
15:13). Here we apprehend an instance of collective suffering that cannot be associated with iniquity, since it was ordained prior to the commission of any sins. Yet Abraham does not protest, as
he does in other instances (see p. 159, about Abraham requesting suffering).

Why is the affliction of enslavement accepted
without question? Perhaps, in the very acceptance
of this undeserved punishment, there is a message
regarding suffering in general. Here, the suffering is obviously of value to the long-range prosperity of the people. God's insistence that the Israelites undergo suffering before attaining freedom
has a multifaceted benefit: By going through the
agony of servitude, the people would better understand and appreciate the benefit of freedom, freedom—not only for themselves, but for others who
are in unfortunate circumstances.

Being afflicted and going through pain, the
Israelites would be more sensitive to the pain of
others. Having suffered the separation of husband

from wife and parent from child, they would be more sensitive to the widow and the orphan. Being denied the chance to live comfortably, they would thereby be more sensitive to the suffering of the poor.

Since all these values of caring and sensitivity are essential components of the Torah and are essential to a Torah way of life, God did not want them to be theoretical niceties to which lip-service is paid, but are not practiced effectively on a daily basis. Therefore, subjugating the Israelites, as painful as it was and as much as God endured the pain with them, was a necessary precondition to their being able to sincerely and energetically carry out the Torah mandate concerning the empathy and sensitivity that must be forthcoming to other individuals in adverse circumstances.

Could this all-embracing suffering be logically justified on the basis of any prior action by the people? Very unlikely. But could it be justified as necessary for the growth of the people into exemplars of concern and caring, as indeed the Jewish people have always been? Most definitely.

Is it fair that a few generations go through intense pain so that future generations benefit thereby? In any calculus that focuses on the moment, we would have great difficulty justifying the suffering. But God has no such difficulty, because the ultimate concerns are of greater importance. There is meaning to the suffering, even though that meaning is in the future.

But all these nice explanations and ennobling suggestions suffer from a severe limitation. All this wrestling with the meaning of suffering is futile, because no matter what framework we give to understanding suffering in general, when the time comes to translate this into personal experience, the theoretical falls far short of offering palatable explanations.

Perhaps that is how it should be. Perhaps it is not for us to know why we are meant to suffer some of the agonies and traumas that we experience. Perhaps it is absurd to expect that we can give reasons for innocent children suffering through tremendous pain. Perhaps, at the end of it all, attempting to explain away these bitter realities is even obscene.

17

Logotherapy
on Suffering

It may be helpful to pause at this juncture to present a perspective on suffering that differs somewhat from the Jewish view. This is the perspective on suffering proposed by Viktor Frankl's *logotherapy*, a psychological system rooted in a philosophy that accentuates the primacy of "meaning" in the human endeavor.

Although the logotherapeutic view on suffering differs somewhat from the Judaic, there are some striking similarities. The most significant similarity is the accentuation of the positive in suffering.

I have mixed feelings about presenting logotherapy's views on suffering. I certainly am not suggesting that Judaism needs vindication of its principles and beliefs from other sources; but it does help to know that Judaism's views are not only theologically sound—they are also psychologically beneficial. This is not surprising, but it is useful to accentuate.

Logotherapy sees life as combining good and bad. Life has unconditional meaning—even in suffering and death, which are unavoidable life entities. In spite of all the bad, we are urged to say yes to life. Suffering can be used in a meaningful way and translated into a positive experience. Suffering is a basic component of life; it is naive to think that life can be a series of only joyful experiences. The individual bent on the experience of joy will be unable to find meaning in suffering; such a person has arbitrarily divided life into positive and negative components, with the negative to be avoided rather than confronted.

But avoiding the negative is not a healthful approach. An integrated life must anticipate highs and lows, joy and melancholy, fulfillment and challenge. Since suffering of some sort is unavoidable, it is better to be philosophically ready, and thus psychologically prepared, for the inevitable affliction.

Logotherapeutic thinking states that there is fundamental human suffering, suffering that belongs to life by the very nature and meaning of life. This suffering stems from the frustration of the search for meaning. This suffering, this inner tension aroused by the desire to attain values, is not a pathological phenomenon; it is a true human expression.

The person who suffers from such frustration has, by this very suffering, exercised self-detachment, and has begun to judge matters based on what he or she ought to be. This type of suffering, inherent as it is to the human condition, must be faced realistically, and should not be tranquilized away. Masking the suffering with valium is a form of spiritual euthanasia.

What is the meaning of suffering? The despair associated with suffering is not a function of the suffering itself, but is instead a function of the doubt about the meaningfulness of the suffering. We are ready and willing to shoulder any suffering once its meaning is apparent. There must be a meaning to suffering if there is to be a meaning to life, since all suffering is a definite, unavoidable component of life.

Ultimately, the problem of the meaning of suffering is really the problem of why suffering is necessary. Logotherapy insists that, rather than avoiding guilt, we have the right to be considered guilty and to be responsible. If we are merely the unfortunate victims of circumstances, then we are less than true human beings, and this dims our will to change.

The blows of suffering may be necessary because, without them, the sufferer may sink into spiritual oblivion. These blows may be conceived as the rude awakening to the purpose of our life, to a confrontation with reality. The suffering caused by the existential vacuum is not real suffering; rather, it is a healthy despair that urges one to do something about one's life. We have the right and the responsibility to own up to this type of suffering in a mature and affirmative manner.

In this regard, Frankl suggests that "Suffering is intended to guard man from apathy, from psychic rigor mortis. As long as we suffer we remain psychically alive. In fact, we mature in suffering, grow because of it—it makes us richer and stronger" (Viktor E. Frankl, *The Doctor and the Soul: From Psychotherapy to Logotherapy*, p. 88). This is a powerful psychological statement with potent theological implications.

No one in a healthy frame of mind would seek out suffering; this is masochistic, not normal. Yet there is a suffering from which there is no escape. How are we to handle this? By transcending it or using it for fulfillment. The meaning of suffering may be unknowable, but meaning in the suffering, or meaning in spite of the suffering, can be discovered.

It is ill-advised to run away from what life presents to us. The thrust of our approach should be to transmute all situations of life into affirmative experiences. When unavoidable suffering presents itself, we should transmute the "suffering from" to a "suffering toward," to translate it into a positive experience. Suffering is a basic and potentially affirmative component of life. The right attitude to suffering can give meaning to it.

Frankl offers a clear example regarding the importance of changing the "suffering from" to a "suffering toward"—to rise above the suffering, to elicit meaning from it. It concerns a doctor who consulted him because he could not shake off the severe depression brought on by the death of his wife. Frankl asked the doctor, "What would have happened, doctor, if you had died first and your wife would have had to survive you?" Whereupon he said, "For her this would have been terrible; how she would have suffered." Frankl then interjected, "You see, doctor, such suffering has been spared her, and it is you who have to pay for it by surviving and mourning her." Suddenly the doctor's suffering took on a meaning—in this case, the meaning of a sacrifice. With meaning, the despair and depression brought on by the death of his wife was eased.

It is easy to affirm life when things go well. The challenge for us is to continue in life even when fate takes bad turns. Were we to give up when confronted by pain or a crisis, many lives would be lost unnecessarily, many ideas stifled, and many achievements never realized. The right kind of suffering—not masochistic but necessary suffering, necessary because it is unavoidable—is a genuine human achievement. For it is only human volition that urges us on in our suffering.

Ultimately, it is impossible to explain the necessity of Godly intervention in terms of punishment, because we cannot really know why God has punished us or why God has decided to spare us punishment. We cannot apprehend God's reasons. We are stuck with the questions, some of which have answers. But the questions related to suffering have responses, positive reactions, to reaffirm life (see further, *The Doctor and the Soul: From Psychotherapy to Logotherapy*, op cit.).

The logotherapeutic view on suffering thus offers invaluable insights that enhance our psychological understanding of the dynamics of suffering. This, in turn, serves to sharpen our comprehension of the Judaic approach to illness and suffering.

18

Can We Have Control?

Many people, in wrestling with illness, find it difficult to accept that they cannot control life. The truth is that we cannot control life even in the best of times. People may think that when they are healthy, it is simply because they have done all that is necessary to ensure this. People who are ill may think that the illness has been caused by a dramatic change, that some foreign demon has entered the system and is taking over.

But the presumption that when one is in health, one is in full control, is as erroneous as the presumption that when one is ill, one has totally lost control. We may do all that we can to ensure our good health, but in the end, good health is a gift—a gift that is precarious at best, because at any moment, something may happen to change everything. One may slip on the ice and break a hip; one may be walking across the street, be hit by a drunk driver, and become crippled for life. A germ may enter one's system, thereby causing a debilitating illness.

Granted, some of these are unlikely occurrences, but to presume at any point in time that we have full control is an illusion. On the other hand, the idea that once we have become sick we have totally lost control is likewise erroneous. We do control the attitude we take toward our situation; we control whether we will allow the illness to ruin our perspective on life, whether it will change us from happy and optimistic to depressed, melancholy, and pessimistic, or whether we fight the disease to whatever extent possible and make the best out of life.

We always have choices, although sometimes these choices may become constricted. In the end, however, we are judged on what we did with the choices that were presented to us, not with choices that were totally beyond our reach.

This point is illustrated in the famous story of Reb Zusya, who expressed anxiety about his great confrontation in heaven, where he would have to answer for his life. He mused that if he were asked why he was not like our Patriarch, Abraham, he would say simply, "I was not Abraham." If he were asked why did he not measure up to our teacher Moses, he would simply say, "Because I was not Moses." But as to the question why he did not measure up to Reb Zusya, that he was very fearful of being asked, because he did not know whether he could answer it adequately. We, too, are not expected to be what we are not, but we are certainly called upon to be what we can be.

What matters are under human control? Heat and cold, in the view of the Talmud, are in the hands of the human being (*Ketuvot* 30a); all else is in the hands of Heaven (God). "Heat and cold" is a metaphor for the human ability and responsibility to avoid danger, to avoid excesses of heat and cold that will undermine health. By logical extension, anything that we can do to preserve our health is within our province of control.

Does this mean that by our behavior we affect how long we will live? This is a complicated question, because either answer poses some difficulty.

If the answer is yes, that our behavior directly affects our longevity, what are we to make of the notion of pre-destination, that we have a specifically allocated number of years, apparently no matter what we do? If the answer is no, that our behavior has no effect on our longevity, then why are we urged to take care of ourselves (see p. 49)?

The answer, therefore, is not either yes or no; the answer is yes *and* no. The matter is clarified in the following discussion.

> "There is a time to be born and a time to die," (Kohelet 3:2). From the time of birth the time of death is predestined. For from the time that a person is born it is decreed how many years that person will live. If that person is meritorious, the person will live out the full complement of years, and if the person is not meritorious, years will be deducted from the full complement . . . . This

is the view of Rabbi Akiva, but the Sages state that
if a person is meritorious they may even add on
to the person's allotted years, and if the person is
not meritorious, then years will be deducted from
the allotment (*Kohelet Rabbah* 3:4; see also *Yevamot*
49b–50a).

Whatever view one takes, it is clear that one's
behavior affects the previously fixed destiny. Rabbi
Akiva suggests that we cannot add to our destiny,
but can diminish it; the Sages insist that we can
add or diminish. Thus, there is a destiny for the
individual, but there is also a partnership within
that destiny. It is not fixed; it fluctuates. The fluc-
tuation is according to the person's merit. That
merit undoubtedly comprises many components,
including taking care of oneself, if there is to be
the expectation of living longer.

In the final analysis, longevity is a matter of
destiny (*Mo'ed Katan* 28a), and that can be changed
for the better, but it takes great merit (*Yevamot* 50a,
starting with the words *moseefeen lo*).

Further regarding control, it should be recognized that we deal with disease on two levels.
There is the simple level, the disease level, for
which we should pursue the best medical attention available. But there is also a second level, that
of uneasiness, anxiety, the apprehensive feelings
that are associated with our being unwell.

The physician may help to put the patient at
ease, and certainly family and friends can encour-
age, inspire, and invigorate the patient. In the end,
though, this, too, is in our hands. It is in the hands

of the person with the disease to decide whether this disease will also cause unease.

Generally, people deal much better with diseases or sicknesses that are transitory, that may even be painful, but for which there is a definite light at the end of the hospital tunnel. For example, people who have difficulties with the heart but are fully aware that following bypass surgery they will be back to full functionality can usually deal with the situation.

On the other hand, those who have a cardiac condition that does not allow for any surgical intervention and who, because of this, must alter their lifestyle and cut down on things that they love to do will have greater difficulty.

Similarly, someone who is wrestling with a very painful sciatic nerve problem and has difficulty walking, but for whom there is a good prospect that surgery will alleviate this pain, is better able to cope than someone who has had a paralytic stroke and has very little hope of gaining full function.

The Torah has much to say about how to deal with pain. The Talmud (*Avot* 6:4) states that the way of Torah is to live a life of pain. This is not to indicate that pain is a must; only that Torah, commitment to God's word and God's way, should be so vital and invigorating that one is able to endure any pain when it comes. We should not seek the pain, but when and if the pain finds us, we should be ready to transcend it.

It is interesting that the rabbinic remedy for many maladies is to occupy oneself with Torah.

Whether a person is suffering from a headache or from any other bodily pain, the talmudic advice is to occupy oneself with Torah study (*Eruvin* 54a).

What is behind this advice? Presumably, the idea behind this is that whenever one focuses directly on one's pain, that pain is likely to become worse rather than better. The best way to transcend the pain is to occupy oneself with useful, worthwhile activity. This is expressed in the Talmud by the strong recommendation to occupy oneself with the Torah as a way to get beyond the pain. By concentrating on other things—and what better thing than Torah?—it is to be hoped that one will forget about the aching head, the hurting arm, or the growling stomach. This is one of the best ways of easing the malaise that afflicts the individual.

Concentrating on other things will also likely alleviate the pain, but concentrating on Torah will do more than alleviate the pain; it will inculcate a sense of transcending purpose and commitment to learn more of God's word. That will likewise imbue the person with a sense of enduring meaning to life that will make the pain more bearable. Therein resides our ultimate control.

19

How Good Is
the Good Life?

For many people, the definition of a good life is one
that is full of pleasant and happy times, and free
from any affliction. There are some interesting and
challenging observations on this matter in classical
Jewish sources.

One observation regards Abraham's request
to God for older age and for affliction. Abraham
apparently argued that had God not given content-
ment to the generation of the flood, they would
not have angered God and rebelled against God,
to which God agreed (*Midrash Tanhuma*, Noah 14).
Affliction started with Abraham.

Another midrashic tradition maintains that,
in fact, it was Isaac who demanded suffering. He
pleaded with God, arguing as follows:

"Sovereign of the universe, when a person dies
without previous suffering, the attribute of judg-

ment is stretched out against that person, but if
You cause the person to suffer, the attribute of
judgment will not be stretched out against that
person." Said the Holy One, blessed is God, to
Isaac: "By your life, you have asked well and I will
commence with you."

Thus, suffering is not mentioned from the beginning of the book until here: "And it came to pass
that when Isaac was old and his eyes were dim . . . ,"
(Genesis 27:1).

It was Isaac's son, Jacob, who demanded illness, saying to God:

"Sovereign of the universe, if one dies without
previous illness, one does not settle one's affairs
with one's children, but if one is ill for two or
three days, that would create the opportunity
to settle one's affairs with the children." Said the
Holy One, blessed is God, to Jacob: "By your life,
you have asked well, and with you it will commence . . . ," and it was told to Joseph, "Behold—
your father is sick" (Genesis 48:1) (*Midrash Rabbah*, Genesis 65:4; see also *Bava Mezia* 87a).

The immediate implication of this midrashic con-
versation is that it was only through the entreaty
of Isaac and Jacob that suffering and illness were
brought into the world.

Jacob asked God's "mercy" to bring sickness
into being. This comes as a rude shock to a world
that goes out of its way to avoid pain, and that
would gladly embrace illness-free life as an ideal.
Why did Jacob ask for illness?

According to Rashi (*Bava Mezia* 87a), this was so that Jacob would have ample time to command and instruct the family before passing on. Jacob was not asking for himself only; obviously he felt that although it is possible for people to share their abiding concerns with their family before they die—even in the absence of illness—it is nevertheless in the nature of human beings to procrastinate.

For Jacob, the importance of parents instructing future generations as to what is proper and what is priority takes precedence over the pain and the agony of illness. Illness may be painful for the moment, but a generation that goes on without direction is painful in an ultimate and, unfortunately, enduring sense.

One may question why God adhered to Jacob's request. The simple answer is that the request was reasonable. This means that God could have rejected the request, but chose instead to grant it.

However, one can make a distinction between illness and suffering. It is possible for people to be ill, but not to suffer. Suffering is associated with pain; illness is associated with weakness. It is true that one who is weak may feel the pain of not being able to achieve what was previously attainable, but that is more a mental anguish that arises from unfulfilled desires than physical pain.

In defense of Jacob, even though the classic translation suggests that Jacob asked for illness, the more precise reading is that Jacob asked for weakness (*hulsha*), the sense that life is ebbing away and death is near. Even though the talmudic comment regarding Jacob's request is linked to the verse wherein it is reported to Joseph that his father Jacob is "ill" (Genesis 48:1), it is quite conceivable that the illness referred to is the illness of becoming weak just before dying. The classic Onkelos translation of the word *holeh* (ill) strongly suggests this interpretation.

However, even if we find a way to defend Jacob, it is not easy to dismiss Abraham and Isaac's requests for affliction. There is little room to interpret this plea in any way other than that expressed by these Patriarchs. What do we make of this?

Perhaps the Midrash is conveying the idea that, deep down, even though we suffer from affliction, we do recognize that suffering does benefit us. The momentary protest is just that—a spontaneous cry from the heart that is not a protest against the need for suffering, but is instead an understandable human reflex.

Sifri (Voet'hanan 6:5) states explicitly that a person should be happier with affliction than with a life of effervescent goodness, because if one is in good circumstances all the days of one's life, then there is no forgiveness for any sin that may have been committed. Through what process is sin pardoned and forgiven? Through affliction, says Sifri.

This view is also expressed in *Midrash Tanhuma* (Yitro 16), where it is stated that a person should be happier with affliction than with the good, for if a person enjoys the good throughout life, then that person's sins have not been forgiven. How are they forgiven? They are forgiven through affliction.

This is an upside-down view of things that puts matters in balance. As this book has stated often, we obviously should not run after suffering, but we also should not be too excited about an overabundance of good. Too much good is no good; or, more precisely, what is good in the short run may not be good in the long run, and what is not good in the short run may be good in the long run.

Concerning a life, or even a period of life, devoid of complication, the Talmud (*Arakhin* 16b) states: "It was taught in the academy of Rabbi Yishmael: Anyone who has gone forty days without suffering has already received his world (reward)."

Ramban (Nahmanides), in *The Gate of Reward* (*Sha'ar HaGmul*, pp. 443–444), explains that:

The purport of this statement relates to the steady changes customary in the world which affect all people. For example, he may find trouble in his work at certain times, and his body will ache when eating certain bad foods unsuitable to his nature. His head too [will ache] when he stands in the sun. Such things cause him wearisome labor and befall even kings. Only a thoroughly wicked person destined for Gehenna is saved from these [molestations], for he is receiving his reward in this world and is being protected by Heaven so that he may do his entire will in this world .... Thus you find that this "trial" constitutes a principle of goodness. Through it, man receives reward and the Name of the Holy One, blessed be He, is exalted. He thus lets it be known to what extent the love and fear of God have pervaded the heart of His servants, how they were drawn after His commandments, and [how they] performed His will as if it was their own (p. 446).

The Midrash makes an analogy between the type of suffering that is inflicted upon the people by God and that which a parent inflicts upon the child (*Midrash Rabbah*, Shemot 1:1). Examples are the failure of Abraham to adequately admonish his son Ishmael, and the failure of Isaac to admonish his son Esau. Both Ishmael and Esau went on to lives of delinquent and wayward behavior. The same is true of Absalom, who was not sufficiently reprimanded by his father David.

The failure of a parent to so instruct and even severely reprimand the child is not an indication of parental love; it is, on the contrary, an indication of parental apathy. God's failure in this regard would also be indicative of apathy. If God were apathetic, this would indicate lack of caring for the individual. Being neglected by God is the ultimate punishment. The fact that one suffers because of God's concern is to be cherished, and to be translated in a positive way.

A father who chastises his son causes his son to love him more. On the scriptural words "but he that loves him chastises him at times" (Proverbs 13:24), it is noted that "because he chastises him at times, therefore does he love him" (*Midrash Rabbah*, Exodus 1:1). Chastising, it must be noted, is not abusing; it is instructing within the framework of love and concern.

Rabbi Eliezer Papo, reflecting rabbinic tradition as presented here, states that there are many types of affliction and that all of them are desirable, for if a person were to sit one's entire days in tranquility, there would be no atonement for any of that person's sins; affliction, in other words, purges the individual's sins. This is contingent on the proviso that the affliction is accepted with love, with the recognition that it atones for one's iniquities (*Pele Yo'etz* p. 289).

If even no minor difficulties come in a person's way over a protracted period of time, this is not a good sign; in fact, it is just the opposite. Thus, those who complain that things never go smoothly, or other words to that effect, should contemplate that a perfectly smooth life is not to be desired. Obviously, this does not mean that one should deliberately set out to make things less than smooth.

On the other hand, unexpected set-backs and unforeseen hurdles are part of life—indeed, a good part of life, because it augurs well for the future. It is better for us not to take things for granted.

It should be noted that one should not deliberately create difficulties for oneself and then consider it as a sign that one is deserving. One cannot create an obstacle and then call it a divine visitation. An affliction is a divine visitation only when it comes from beyond the person, not when it is engineered by the person. In other words, we are not to play games with our relationship to God; we are deluding ourselves if we do so. Instead, we must do our best—whether in terms of our ordi-

nary daily activities or in the pursuit and mainte-
nance of our health—to wrestle with whatever ills
come our way in the best manner possible.

  We must, to the best of our abilities, do good
things in life. At the same time, however, we should
never become addicted to the "good life." Over
the long haul, what seems good may not be, and
what appears to be bad may actually be good.

20

Attitudes Toward Suffering

The importance of maintaining the proper attitude to suffering is highlighted in a comment of the Rabbis regarding Job (*Pesikta*, sec. 47, Aharay Mot). It is suggested that in the regular prayers, when we make mention of the God of Abraham, Isaac, and Jacob, the God of Job ought to have been included. However, because when affliction hit him Job started to balk and to question God, his name is not included in these prayers. This illustrates the importance of dealing favorably and affirmatively with suffering as a dominant motif in Jewish life. Dealing appropriately with suffering puts one on par with the Patriarchs—no small feat.

On the other hand, we do have a full measure of understanding for those who make untoward remarks in the throes of suffering. "One is not held responsible for what one says in the hour of one's distress," states Rava (*Bava Batra* 16b).

We understand Job's reaction. However, it is one thing to understand a reaction, and quite another to find that reaction worthy of emulation. We understand Job, and can even relate to him; but we cannot raise him to the status of role model.

A fundamental attitudinal principle in suffering, painful as it may be, is that whatever suffering is visited upon the person either is deserved and intended for ultimate good, or is a way of making a good person even better. Again, this does not necessarily mean that the suffering person is a deficient human being; we all have room for improvement.

Consider the talmudic statement that for three sins women die in childbirth: the failure to properly observe the laws of menstruation, *hallah*, and the kindling of the *Shabbat* lights (*Shabbat* 31b). This is one of numerous statements in the Talmud that tries to link a calamity to some precipitant cause. One wonders why there is such a harsh punishment for these lapses.

A hint is offered by Rabbi Yisrael Lipshitz in his commentary *Tiferet Yisrael*. Regarding childbirth, the author remarks that this is a time of danger when calamity can strike. *Tiferet Yisrael* offers the intriguing observation that the three aforementioned obligations rest upon the woman, and are also binding on others, who rely on her to take care of these concerns.

This explanation offers an interesting insight into the Mishnah's statement. The point here is not merely the failure to adhere to a commandment; it is the failure to live up to one's responsibility, especially when others are dependent upon the one to carry it out.

The Sages thus saw dying in childbirth as probably having been caused by this dereliction of responsibility. This was their way of sending a message to one who wants to be a parent and to actualize the responsibility towards the child. The child, in order to develop, needs a responsible parent. The failure to be responsible in other areas is indicative of a flawed perception of duty and responsibility. Maybe such irresponsible people are not deserving of being parents.

This is tough medicine to swallow, but the message that the Sages tried to convey is quite clear: Nothing happens without cause, a cause that makes what unfolds a justified reaction.

I have often been asked to justify this statement by people who argue that there are many people who do not adhere to these obligations and yet seem to have no difficulty in childbirth. This is a legitimate question, but the answer is already anticipated in the commentary of *Tiferet Yisrael*.

This punishment occurs only when others rely upon the woman to carry out these obligations for them, and the woman is not careful in her observance of the laws. Obviously, when both husband and wife fail to observe the laws of menstruation, the taking of *hallah*, and *Shabbat*, then this entire matter is inapplicable to them.

On the presumption that all suffering is warranted, Nahmanides raises a profound question concerning the attitude to suffering.

You may pose this question; "Since the Sages established these methods [of reward and punishment] according to their intention and the preponderance of the verses in the Torah and [the books of] the prophets, why then do the prophets complain about this matter?"

Nahmanides responds that "The prophets' statements about this matter and their complaints about this state of affairs were [analogous] to the utterances of a sick man who is vexed over his illness and exaggerates about it. He cries out because of the great trouble and pain [which afflict him, expressing shock] about why this befell him and [wondering] how it is possible to survive his great trouble. That is to say, the prophets wonder before the Holy One, Blessed be He, and say before Him: 'Master of the Universe! Why do You conduct Yourself according to this principle? We end our days in terror while these wicked ones who stretch forth their hand against Your sacred habitation live in peace and tranquillity in the world.' [The prophets make these protestations] although they know that the principle is true and the judgement is righteous" (Nahmanides, *The Gate of Reward*, translated by Chavel, pp. 449, 451–452).

This is a human, and humane, reflex of those who are sensitive to the pain experienced by others. We know the ultimate answer, yet we ask the immediate question. We must ask it, or else we become desensitized to human agony. But we likewise must respond in a life-affirming way, lest we let the suffering break our spirit.

Rabbi Dov, the Maggid of Mezeritch, illustrates the impact of suffering with the story of a child who was playing a rough game with a group of his playmates when a thorn became embedded in his foot

(*Yalkut Sipurim*). At that moment, his father appeared and told him to come with him so that he could remove the thorn.

The child, however, who at the moment felt no pain and was afraid of the pain that would be caused to him by the removal of the thorn, refused. The father, undeterred, took hold of the child and forcibly removed the thorn from his foot.

The father then shared with his son the following reproof: "My son, it is true that removing the thorn caused you more pain than leaving it in the foot. But if I had not removed it, the wound in your foot would have festered; it would have hurt much more, and it would have been much harder to cure." God is, thus, cruel to be kind, and suffering can often be a blessing in disguise.

One of the major messages in Jewish thought on suffering is that it may be a blessing in disguise. But it is a blessing only if we translate it properly; otherwise, it can be a debilitating curse. Rabbenu Bahya thus explains that when Rabbi Akiva said that suffering is precious, he meant that it was precious only because of the submission involved; that with this virtue a person will attain the most profound Godly desire (*Kad HaKemah*, under the category of *hakhna'ah*).

Suffering, then, with all its travail, is an opportunity. What we make of that opportunity is a defining component of our lives. It is not a defiling component.

Rabbenu Bahya further states that suffering is intended as an atonement for sins. The suffering is visited upon a person to purge that person's sins, so that the person will be totally meritorious for the future world. Therefore God imposes suffering on the righteous for their relatively small number of sins, in the transitory time of this world that has no permanence.

The suffering is visited upon the least significant part of the person—the body—in order to make the person meritorious, and to bestow upon that person the fruits of his or her good deeds in the most glorious of times (the World-to-Come) and in the most exalted part of the person (the soul) (*Kad HaKemah*, under the category of *kippurim* (1)).

RaN expounds on why the Sages praised suffering. Whomever God desires, God crushes in suffering; in other words, God acts with mercy toward God's creations by bringing suffering upon them, since their instinct to do wrong is weakened, and they become more desirable to God. This is what is referred to as an affliction of love. Even if a righteous person never sins, and fulfills all of the commandments, it is impossible for such a person not to have some block to the total embrace of God. Therefore, God occasionally brings suffering on the righteous even though they have not fallen into the trap of sinfulness, merely to further distance them from matters of this world (*Derashot HaRaN*, drush 10).

This puts quite a positive theoretical face on suffering. No one can be sure as to the reason for the suffering being endured, but the fact that there are positive facets to it should be of great benefit in developing a constructive approach to it.

Embracing the appropriate approach to illness and suffering is more than mere advice. According to a major expositor of the obligatory commandments:

> The person is commanded to justify that which has occurred, whether it is to the body or to one's offspring or to one's possession. This is in line with the verse, "You should know with your heart, that in the same way as a person admonishes his son, so God admonishes you" [Deuteronomy 8:5]. One should establish this in the heart and bow the heart and accept in silence. Do not say that you are more righteous than God, and do not attribute this to chance, because then God will leave your entire life to chance. Rather the person should investigate the deeds that were carried out and repent. This is a main component of the commandment to love God, which includes that one love God with all one's might. The Sages [see *Berakhot* 54a] expounded that this refers to any measure by which God metes out to the individual, whether it is in good measure, or via suffering, that it should be accepted with joy (*Sefer Haredim*, affirmative commandments derived from the Torah that are contingent on the heart, 1:31).

To accept suffering with joy is a tall order. But from a psychological viewpoint, it is a superior approach to any alternative. From a theological approach, it is more consistent with any of the possible reasons for why God has caused this suffering to unfold, all of which are geared to the benefit rather than the detriment of the afflicted righteous individual.

Consistent with this general attitude, Maharal explains the Talmud's view on how to approach one's suffering (*Berakhot* 5a; see p. 142). When one is overcome by affliction, one should first assume that one has done something wrong; that is to say, to search one's deeds, because wrongdoing signifies a deficiency in the person. However, if one cannot find a logical connection, the next step is to link it to failure to occupy oneself with Torah. Failure to occupy oneself with Torah does not involve a deficiency in the individual; rather, the individual is lacking because there was an opportunity for fulfillment that was not realized. However, if this also does not explain matters, then the person should assume that these are afflictions of love. In Maharal's explanation, afflictions of love are intended to dislodge the person from any materialistic affirmations, thereby enabling the person to reach the highest level. The suffering a person endures removes any material deficiencies and leads to a perfect purification.

But, as Maharal goes on to explain, this can work only if the person accepts this in love, because, failing that, there is no clinging to God. How could these then be afflictions of love?

It becomes clear, from Maharal's explanation, that whether or not an affliction can qualify as an affliction of love is a dialectic. It is not enough that it was so intended by God; it also must be so translated by the person. In other words, it takes two to establish the nature of the suffering.

Maharal goes on to explain that this is what the Talmud means by the statement that afflictions cannot be of love if they involve an inability to occupy oneself with Torah because Torah is a prime way of clinging to God. The same is true of the view that if these afflictions do not allow the individual to pray, they cannot be afflictions of love, since they, too, create a distance when they should bring about closeness.

In the end, however, even these two situations are considered afflictions of love. Even if they cause disruptions of preoccupation with Torah or with prayer, nevertheless the afflictions do purge the individual and ultimately will achieve a higher purpose (Maharal, *Netiv HaYisurin*, Chap. 1).

The benefits of developing the appropriate approach to suffering, and, indeed, the proper approach to life—being satisfied with one's portion, no matter what that portion may be (*Avot* 4:1)—are elucidated in the explanation of the behavior of the great Sage Hillel.

The Talmud extols Hillel's great virtue (*Shabbat* 31a)—that he was happy even in his suffering and accepted it with a cheerful countenance. He also taught the members of his household to behave the same way. Therefore, when he heard the sound of screams in the city, he said that he was sure that they did not emanate from his household (*Berakhot* 60a). Shelah explains that Hillel was expressing not blind faith, but logical confidence that his household would endure any travail with a good heart and would not have screamed. This was because Hillel had taught them the proper attitude to adversity.

Shelah points out the instructive analogy of the sale of Joseph, which at the time seemed to be a tragic happening, but in the end turned out to be the reason and the process by which he became a powerful person, the second-in-command in Egypt (Shelah, *Asarah Ma'amarot*). In other words, suffering can be transmuted from affliction to opportunity, depending on our resolve to make the most of the situation.

Another thought that helps develop a constructive, affirmative attitude to suffering is the pervasiveness of suffering, and that no matter how bad things are, they could be even worse.

Rabbi Eliezer Papo makes a few observations pertinent to the issue of illness. He suggests that it helps us to be aware that for every bad circumstance, including illness; for every missing element, such as health; matters could always be worse, and that in itself should be a source of comfort.

Everyone suffers. We are in good company: The great luminaries of each generation, including Abraham, Isaac, Jacob, Joseph, Aaron the great Kohen, Samuel, David, all suffered.

In reality, there is no complete good in this world, and there is no one who does not endure some ill or some deficiency. Whatever does befall us we should accept, and we should pronounce blessing on the bad and on the good (*Pele Yo'etz* on *Hoser*, p. 253).

In pronouncing blessing, we ourselves become blessed. We can transmute the "suffering from" to a "suffering toward," to give meaning to the suffering as instrumentality for spiritual growth, and to thereby make suffering a blessing.

21

Attitudes
Toward Death

Although this book is about Judaism on illness
and suffering, not about Judaism on death, nevertheless it is almost unavoidable to touch upon the
Judaic attitude to death.

The attitude to death, in Judaism, is surpris-
ingly positive. We do not seek out death; rather
we incorporate the reality of death into life. Midrashic comment on the verse, "And God saw everything that God had made, and behold it was very
good" (Genesis 1:31), suggests that "very good" can
be equated with death (*Midrash Rabbah*, Genesis 9:5).

In a similar vein, it is said of the psalmist King
David that "he looked upon the day of death and
broke into song" (*Berakhot* 10a). We are thus presented with a positive outlook on death within a
faith system that accentuates an affirmative attitude to life and a sacred obligation to affirm and
enhance life (see Chapter 6).

These two ideas can be reconciled with the mediating principle that we would not be faced with the imperative to act and to accomplish if life were endless. The fact that existence may be terminated suddenly is a reality that forces us—or ought to force us—to utilize the allotted moments as meaningfully as possible.

It seems, though, that the attitude to death in the abstract is not deemed sufficient for influencing one's behavior. Thus, to prevent transgression, the Talmud proposes a proactive integration of awareness of one's inevitable demise, that one be mindful of where one is eventually going—to a place of dust, worms, and maggots (*Avot* 3:1). It is said of the righteous that they "set their death in the forefront of their thoughts" (*Midrash Rabbah*, Ecclesiastes 7:9).

A famous Sage, in order to bring home the importance of the awareness of death, suggested to his disciples that they repent one day before their death. He was immediately confronted with the obvious question: "Does, then, one know on what day one will die?" To which the Sage responded; "Then all the more reason that one repent today, lest one die tomorrow, and thus one's entire life is spent in repentance" (*Shabbat* 152a).

Repentance is presented here in the existential sense, as a constant process of investigating the past to improve the future. Judaism links the unavoidable fact of death with the possibilities for a meaningful life. It is dangerous to propose that one must be constantly mindful of death, as this can easily lead to neurotic behavior; it is more realistic to balance this extreme against the other extreme of neglect. Each person must strike his or her own unique balance. This balance of the awareness of death is achieved when one establishes the "game plan" for life, and infuses one's life with meaning and purpose.

In the words of *Midrash Rabbah* (Ecclesiastes 8:17), "Death is near to you and far from you, as well as far from you and near you." The more one is interested in merely keeping the self alive, the more one cuts off the self from meaningful living. In the pursuit of years, we waste the days; but the more we realize that we are mortal and destined to die, the more we will try to accomplish, thus perhaps even gaining immortality. Death, properly understood, can be a vital, life-enhancing force.

This approach to death is consistent with the attitude to suffering, insofar as it accentuates the positive and focuses on transforming a potentially traumatic reality into a meaningful reality that meaningfully affirms life.

Any understanding of the Jewish concept of death is incomplete, even misleading, without incorporating into the discussion the concept of the World-to-Come, (*olam haba*). The concept of *olam haba* not only is related to death; it is also intricately bound to the understanding of illness and suffering. This matter is discussed in a separate chapter (Chapter 23).

VI

ULTIMATE HOPE

22

What Is Suffering?

Our notion of suffering reflexively associates suffering with pain. Most of us usually can handle unfulfilled expectations, but we are in dread of pain. Escape from pain is perhaps one of the biggest industries in modern times. Pain relievers and painkillers find their way into almost every human body at some point; they are used for everything from headaches to broken bones to cancer.

Within Judaism, however, the parameters are somewhat different. We refuse to view suffering as an accident. We see suffering as having a potentially constructive purpose, because we understand it as divine visitation. It is, in one form or another, a wake-up call. The word most often used to describe suffering is not *tsaar*. *Tsaar* is pain. Suffering is called *yisurin*. *Yisurin* are chastisements that may not even be very painful, but are alarms to wake us from spiritual slumber.

Since we view suffering as a wake-up call, then the definition of suffering as Godly visitation is expanded to include any intrusion on tranquility or expectation that may be construed as a wake-up call. There is an illuminating talmudic discussion of this matter that makes sense only within this framework.

The Talmud (*Arakhin* 16b) expounds:

At what stage is a visitation considered a chastisement? Rabbi Elazar states if one, for example, had a garment woven and it does not fit. Rabah the younger—or, as some say, Rabbi Ze'ira, and as others say, Rabbi Shmuel son of Nahmani—raised the following objection: "Was not more than this said, that even if it had been intended to serve him hot wine and he was served cold wine, or it was intended to be served cold and it was served to him hot, that too is accounted as a divine visitation, and you say only at that stage?" Mar the son of Ravina said: "Even if one's shirt gets turned inside out." Rabah—others say Rav Hisda, or, again, as some others say, Rabbi Yitzhak, and still others state that it was taught—said: "Even if one puts the hand into the pocket to take out three coins and takes out only two. But this is only the case where one indeed intended to take out three and took out two, but not if the person meant to take out two and three came into the hand, because it is no trouble to throw it back." But why all this discussion? Because it was taught in the school of Rabbi Yishmael—Anyone upon whom forty days have passed without divine visitation has received his world.

There is a two-pronged message in this talmudic passage. One, as previously elucidated, is that affliction covers an entire range of circumstances, including those that we look upon as minor annoyances. These, too, are Godly messages, and they contain potential meaning, contingent on our taking these annoyances as interventions.

The other message, elaborated upon earlier (see Chapter 19), is that a life free of glitches and devoid of wake-up calls is not as desirable as it seems. If no difficulties are visited on a person, this indicates that the person may be a lost cause, someone for whom any visitation is a waste of God's time and energy.

Of all the afflictions a person may receive, one stands out. "Rabbi Hiyya states that all affliction is hard, but the affliction of poverty is the worst of all. All afflictions that come, when they leave, the person is as new as before the affliction visitation, but the affliction of poverty weakens the eyes of the individual. Recovery is not possible" (*Yalkut Shimoni*, Ruth, Chap. 1, 601). To this day, poverty is the most critical factor affecting health and longevity.

Poverty is also a challenge that must be addressed by the entire community, which has a sacred obligation to help extricate the poverty-stricken from their plight (see, for example, Leviticus 25:35; Deuteronomy 15:7–8). We dare not use as an excuse the fact that poverty is a divine visitation that is needed and deserved. We can and must do our best to properly understand the meaning of God's actions, but we dare not play God.

23

The *Olam Haba* Factor

No analysis of Judaism on illness and suffering is worthy of credibility without fully integrating the concept of *olam haba*, the World-to-Come, into the equation.

One of the problems associated with wrestling with evil and suffering in this world is that we pose this question concerning evil and suffering—which is obviously a question of theodicy—as if it is a matter of personal suffering in this world only. We fail to take into account the long range—life beyond this world.

To address the issue of suffering from a Jewish perspective without taking *olam haba* into account is inadequate, and, in fact, is intellectually absurd. The ultimate explication of the meaning of human life is in the World-to-Come. Trying to understand illness and suffering without the *olam haba* is akin to attempting to explain how the Earth functions without considering the roles of the sun and the moon. The result will be incomplete, as well as nonsensical.

The *olam haba* factor weighs quite heavily in the Judaic approach to death. The idea is that this world is only a vestibule leading up to the main palace, the World-to-Come. The Talmud exhorts us to prepare in this world—in the vestibule—to be worthy of the palace (*Avot* 4:21).

Death, aside from the positive impact it may have on life, is also, if properly understood, not the end, but rather a transitory phase leading to the ultimate mode of existence. The notion of a future beyond the here-and-now finds its way into the classic Jewish ethical treatise, *Pirkay Avot*, as does the preamble to each summertime week's study of this great work. That preamble speaks of everyone having a share in the future (see Reuven P. Bulka, *Chapters of the Sages: A Psychological Commentary on Pirkey Avoth*, Northvale, N.J.: Jason Aronson, 1993, pp. 15–16). In a sense, ethics itself is contingent on the future focus; contingent on realizing the importance of ultimate rather than transitory truth, on Godly rather than human, and therefore selectively subjective values.

In the Judaic scheme of things, one is visited with suffering in this world in order to be purged of all wrong or to be spiritually fine-tuned, and thereby to be eligible for and ready to enter into an eternal future. Is this punishment?

In a world devoid of any future, where the present is all that counts, this is punishment, indeed. In reality, we have inflicted this upon ourselves by our tacit refusal to allow the concept of a future beyond this world into our operative psyche. This is unfortunate, because once we do that, then all the explanations we give for our suffering are exercises in futility and chicanery; they simply do not work. They become secular explanations for religious concerns, psychological jargon that projects as some sort of pseudotheology.

It is only because we have an eye toward a future beyond this world that we can endure. But endure we have done over the course of the generations because, at least until this generation, the concept of *olam haba,* the world beyond this world, was an essential part of Judaic thought. Even in our generation, the fact that deeply religious people seem to endure suffering more resolutely than others is directly related to the idea of *olam haba*, and the understanding that the suffering may be a gift from God to help people ready themselves for this eternal spiritual life.

Consider a person who is about to undergo serious surgery—for example, a coronary bypass. The physicians tell the person that after the bypass it will be possible to resume a normal life. Heretofore, because of the prevailing problems, every movement caused pain, and every attempt at vigorous activity brought with it total failure. Is the person willing to go through with the surgery?

Under normal circumstances, given the promise that following the surgery and the pain associated with it and the rehabilitation process the person will be able to live a normal life, there is not only a willingness, but even an eagerness to go through with the operation. In the end, it is the focus on a future beyond the pain that enables one to endure the pain of the moment.

On a broader scale, a person who is aware of a future that will give meaning to the suffering will thereby be able to endure the suffering in this world. Frankl, the astute psychotherapist, realized that if the future beyond this world is cut off from the human perspective, it is virtually impossible to impute an ultimate meaning to suffering. Lacking this perspective, the suffering person has little incentive to endure (see Reuven P. Bulka, *The Quest for Ultimate Meaning: Principles and Applications of Logotherapy*, New York: Philosophical Library, 1979, Chap. 10).

Very often, we despair because we are mired in a predicament from which extrication seems unlikely. Precisely here is where a sharp focus on meaning that exists beyond the moment is so vital. By focusing on the future, we can transcend the present and its frustrations, even if the only future that can be focused on is beyond death.

So, the idea that suffering is associated with our imperfections and geared to inducing a spiritual readiness for the future in *olam haba* is not as drastic and as disturbing as it may appear. Having explained this, however, it is not recommended that we impose this upon a patient in the throes of agony, especially if this concept would be novel to the patient in the midst of the pain.

The notion of suffering in this world as preparatory for the future, for ultimate reality, is a recurring theme in rabbinic writings. The Talmud (*Kiddushin* 40b) states that God brings affliction upon the righteous in this world so that they may inherit *olam haba*, the World-to-Come.

The *Zohar* (Vayeshev 12) strikes a similar chord when it remarks, "Come and see how much bad the righteous endure in this world; evil upon evil and pain upon pain, in order to make them meritorious for *olam haba* [eternal life]." The *Zohar* reiterates this later (Vayeshev 27): "God gives pain to the righteous in this world in order to make the righteous meritorious for *olam haba*."

Another comment from the *Zohar* goes into more detail. "Rabbi Elazar states that all that God does is in justice, in order to purge the soul and bring it to *olam haba*, because all the actions of God are in justice and truth, and in order to remove the *zuhama* [spiritual stain] that the person acquired in this world. There, the body is broken and the soul purifies" (Vayeshev 36).

Later sources support this theme. For example, Rabbenu Bahya asserts that everything God gives a person in this world, whether it be contentedness or suffering, is in the category of kindness and mercifulness of God. Through suffering, the person attains the true and everlasting life of *olam haba*, the future world (*Kad HaKemah*, under the title Purim).

Rabbi Shneur Zalman of Liadi (*Tanya*, the letter on repentance, Chap. 12) says that joy is associated with going through bodily affliction because it is good for the soul of the person who has sinned to purge that sin in this world. The person will thereby be saved from any purging that will be done in the place beyond this world that specializes in this activity, where the exercise would be much more intense and excruciating.

The Talmud relates a fascinating episode (*Sanhedrin* 101a) concerning when Rabbi Eliezer became ill and his students went to visit him. He told them that there was a strong anger (of God against him) in this world. The students started to cry, but Rabbi Akiva started to smile. They asked him: "Why do you smile?" He asked them: "Why do you cry?" They replied: "A *sefer Torah* [Torah scroll, meaning their teacher, Rabbi Eliezer] is in pain, and we should not cry!" Rabbi Akiva told them: "As long as I saw our teacher, that his wine did not go sour, his flax did not get beaten, his oil did not get spoiled, and his honey did not become rancid, I said, 'God forbid, perhaps Rebbe has received his world [reward],' but now that I see that he is in pain, I rejoice." Rabbi Eliezer then asked him: "Akiva, have I failed to fulfill anything in the entire Torah?" Replied Rabbi Akiva: "You have taught us that 'there is no righteous individual on earth who does good and will not sin' [Ecclesiastes 7:20]."

Rabbi Akiva declared suffering to be precious (*Sanhedrin* 101a–b) because it atones. He saw the value of suffering on not only a theoretical level, but a practical level. He was able to address the complicated question of suffering as it relates to sin with the necessary delicacy. We all need wake-up calls, said Rabbi Akiva to his Rebbe based on what his Rebbe had himself taught him.

Our inability to comprehend or apprehend the meaning of the suffering does not mean that because of this there is no meaning to the suffering. In faith, we firmly believe that God has a plan and that God has reasons.

If the pain comes from God, there is a reason for the pain. We would like to believe that God has not merely good reasons, but reasons for the good. That is what faith is all about. Faith does not oblige us to have the answers; faith obliges us to believe that there is an answer.

This, however, depends on a firm belief in a future world, in *olam haba*, where these answers will become clear to us. If we reject *olam haba* and restrict our experience—and, in fact, all existence—to this world only, then our failure to come up with answers is not only frustrating, it is also devastating and psychologically debilitating. If we insist that there is no reality beyond this world, and that all answers must conform to this world, then we are locking ourselves into a box from which there is no escape. There is no future without answers, and there are no answers without a future.

If our faith in God as the ultimate reality and our belief in the ultimate reality of a world beyond this world go hand-in-hand, then it is intellectually shallow to make demands of God on a purely this-worldly basis, when in fact the notion of God, and our existence as linked to God, transcend this world.

Ultimate reality is not merely a theological notion. The conviction regarding ultimate reality

actually pervades the judicial system. So many biblical laws are beyond lower-court enforceability and
are given over to God as Ultimate Judge. Good examples of this are the many ethical imperatives in
Leviticus (Chap. 19) that are punctuated with God's
signature: " . . . I am the Lord."

Many of these ethical imperatives are related
not to deeds, but to thoughts. An earthly court cannot enter a person's mind to decide whether one
deliberately deceived or placed a stumbling block
in front of the blind. Only God knows, and we
leave the judgment concerning these matters to
the "Knower of thoughts."

The judicial system of the Torah is quite ex-
acting. We cannot give out a death sentence for
even a crime of murder unless a forewarning was
given to the perpetrator of the crime that was acknowledged by the perpetrator. Additionally, the
act of murder must be committed in the presence
of two independent, unrelated eyewitnesses.

But if that is the case, then those murderers
who commit homicide in the presence of only one
witness or against whom there is an overwhelming circumstantial case will go free. On the surface, it appears that the killer has gotten away with
murder. No one gets away with anything, however.
The murderer has escaped the hands of justice on
this earth, but we have faith that ultimate justice
will prevail.

The same is true of all that a person must endure in life. It may not seem fair, and there may
be no rational explanation for what has happened,
but we remain firm in our belief that everything

in life will be properly explained in due time. In a future world, everything will ultimately make sense, and people will get what they merit, for better or for worse. This is part and parcel of the faith that we cling to unconditionally, even in the most challenging of times.

24

Realism and Resignation

It goes without saying that when we receive bad news, the diagnosis of a disease within our bodies, the wrong approach is to deny that this is actually happening to us. It is natural to want to deny the tumor or the aneurism because we all want to be healthy and well. But it is not realistic.

Clearly, however, the acceptance of the reality of our illness in no way, shape, or form implies resignation to the consequences of that illness, to the surrendering of life. We can accept that we have cancer or some other debilitating illness, and at the same time resolve to fight with all the tenacity at our disposal to overcome it.

The situation may be fraught with physical pain, which may be out of our control except for the degree to which it can be eased with painkillers. However, the extent to which the pain gives birth to despair is in the hands of the individual.

This is not to make light of any illness—God forbid. It is to place heavy emphasis on empowerment, on the ability of individuals to control their attitude to their infirmity. This attitude affects the entire atmosphere around them, including their relationship with their family and friends.

Family and friends are more likely to gather around a fighter than a complainer. Offering words of encouragement to someone who is despairing of life is not a simple task. Retorts such as, "It's easy for you to say—you don't have my pain," even if unspoken, are commonly thought by those who are ill.

When people sense that they cannot help, they usually back off. This is the beginning of a downward spiral; the crankiness and despair discourage the help of others, thus creating a loneliness that further reinforces the despair.

The message in all this is clear: We create the atmosphere around our situation by the attitude we take toward our predicament, for better or for worse.

25

There Is Always Hope

The one thing that patients wrestling with illness try to hang on to is the hope for improvement— the hope that the disease will disappear, the hope that life will go on, the hope that they will be able to survive.

Of course, terminality—to put it bluntly, death— is the unavoidable destiny of all human beings. No one can expect to live forever. The fact that life must end in no way compromises a person's need to hope. There is always hope. "Even if a sharp sword rests upon one's neck, one should not desist from prayer" (*Berakhot* 10a).

Even in the face of death there is hope, because, in Judaism, death is not the end. Death is merely the end of this worldly existence; it is a passage not merely "from," but also "into." Fundamental to Jewish belief is the conviction that beyond this world is another world, the World-to-Come.

So even if a physician tells a family that their beloved is beyond hope, such a comment must be rejected out of hand. In the context of this-world-liness there may be no hope, but the presumption that all there is to existence is this world is not a Jewish presumption.

There is always hope, because there is always a world beyond this world. Suffering, illness, and death must not be allowed to extinguish the hope—and, indeed, the conviction that infuses this hope—that there is indeed a tomorrow, not only for the family that is losing a loved one, but also for the loved one who is leaving this world.

Because entry into the future world is so important, we should take every opportunity offered to us to make this more likely. We are called upon to save an endangered person on *Shabbat* and to disregard any *Shabbat* restrictions that would stand in the way of this. This rule applies even if it is clear that the person being saved will last only another few minutes.

The logic behind this is that we forego one *Shabbat* so that the person in danger can observe many other *Shabbat* experiences. But why is it that we can forego *Shabbat* even if it is clear that the person in danger will not make it to another *Shabbat*? Because even in the few extra minutes granted to the person being saved, the person can reflect on previous *Shabbat* breaches, repent, and render them retroactively as correctly observed *Shabbat* days (see Exodus 31:16, *Shabbat* 151b, and *Yoma* 85b; *Torah Temimah* of Rabbi Barukh HaLevi Epstein, Exodus 31:16, note 36). In saving a person for a few more minutes, we express our faith in ultimate reality, in the World-to-Come. The few minutes can be a lifetime.

One can genuinely clear the slate of the past, thereby paving the path for the future. There is always hope, because we always have the power to shape our ultimate destiny, even when we may appear to be comatose. (For more on hope, see Maurice Lamm's inspirational volume, *The Power of Hope.*)

VII

BALANCE

26

Why Me? Why Not Me?

The Judaic perspective on suffering presented herein dramatically changes the classic question that has been the focus of many treatises on suffering. That classic question is: "Why me?"

If we take the perspective that having no difficulties whatsoever may be an indication of one's greater failings, the question to be asked by one who has not suffered in life should rather be, "Why not me? What have I done wrong that my life has gone so perfectly?" But hardly anyone ever asks that question.

If everyone is subject to suffering, then why should anyone expect to be the exception? This is not intended to be insulting or degrading; it is merely intended to put a different perspective on the situation. After all, the person who asks, "Why me?" is stating, unfortunately, that everyone else is doing well and only he or she is suffering, and that the suffering is undeserved.

This is not the case, however. The truth is that everyone goes through some form of suffering. That a person should expect to breeze through life without suffering is unrealistic; posed as a theological challenge, it is unfair.

If, as Judaism suggests, all suffering is related to either personal failings that must be corrected or personal growth that must be effected, then questioning the necessity of the affliction becomes an expression of impertinence. This is because the complainer is actually suggesting that the adversity is unneccessary, since there was no need for any corrective intervention by God. In a word, why mess with perfection?

To claim, even implicitly, that one is perfect is sheer arrogance. From both the immediate and the long-range perspective, one is better off wrestling with guilt feelings than living in an illusion of ease that is rooted in arrogance. With guilt, at least the person is in a humble state and is trying to get rid of the demons of the past. That is preferable to the assertion that everything is fine as-is and needs no improvement. That attitude is a most destructive character trait.

27

Complaining and Thanking

Another critical component of illness and suffering is the balance of complaints versus thanks. Take, for example, the act of breathing, which, according to the Talmud (*Yoma* 85a), is important in gauging life.

Rabbi Levi says in the name of Rabbi Hanina that a person must give praise to God for every single breath that is inhaled, because the main source of life is in the breathing process (*Midrash Rabbah*, Genesis 14:11).

In other words, before we rush to complain to God about the things that have not gone well, we must be thankful for those parts of life we normally take for granted, but could not live without. The care that must be taken to ensure that a city's air is clean is evident in such regulations as expressed in Tosefta (*Bava Batra* 1:7), where it is stated that one places the incinerators fifty *amot* (about 75 feet) from the city in order not to pollute the air.

Being in good health—having an energetic system—is considered the best of all blessings (*Yevamot* 102b). In Ecclesiasticus (30:14), Ben Sira states that there is no wealth like good health, and that it is preferable to a life of sickness. The saying is, literally, "Better a poor person in good health than a wealthy person in ill health."

The Jewish way is to wake up each morning with the words of the famous *Modeh ani* on one's lips, thanking God for restoring us to life after having been asleep. In other words, we begin the day with a thank you to God for being alive. Many people mouth this statement as a reflex, but its value inheres in understanding what the statement implies, and integrating this into our psyche.

By integrating this concept into our psyche, we become expressers of gratitude for every good that we experience. But we are not grateful merely for waking up; a complete range of thank-yous are enunciated in the famous blessings that begin the morning prayers—including the fact that there is light, that we can see, that we can walk, and that all our needs are taken care of. These are the well-known *Birkhot HaShahar*, blessings recited first thing in the morning.

Indeed, for everything that has been bestowed upon us, we are obliged to acknowledge God as the source of the blessing and to thank God. That is why there is a blessing for virtually everything in life that we enjoy. If we take inventory of all that we experience in life, the sum total of the good experiences will far outweigh the bad.

The mere fact that we breathe, think, benefit from sight, and feel, and that we do these things on a daily basis, is an overwhelming kindness. We dare not take this kindness for granted, or to pass a day without acknowledging and thanking God for this. If we said all of the thank-yous that are owed to God and sincerely meant it, we would be so overwhelmed with the sheer magnitude of our thanks, and so convinced of the bountiful good that God has given to us, that we would be much more reluctant to complain even when painful, never mind uncomfortable, times invade our lives.

In fact, the Jewish way is for one to give thanks for misfortune as well as for good fortune, as it is stated: "You should love the Lord your God with all your heart and with all your soul and with all your might" (Deuteronomy 6:5)—meaning whatever measure God metes out to you, good or bad (*Berakhot* 54a). If we recall that suffering is intended for the ultimate good, then there is, indeed, much for which to be appreciative.

Concerning complaining to God for all that has gone wrong, there are those who suggest that it is perfectly acceptable to complain to God about this (see Shmuel Boteach, *Wrestling with God: A Jewish Response to Suffering*). Even accepting the proposition that it is acceptable to protest and to complain to God, this very process must be placed into context.

Consider a woman who goes out of her way to do everything for the family and who, despite a tremendous workload of her own, makes sure that the house is clean and that the meals are nutritious and filling. On one occasion, she serves food that is a bit overdone. One of the family members complains about this, challenging the cook and her abilities.

If the family members never express their thanks for all of the nice things that are done for them and are only verbal when it is time to complain, then the wrong that they have committed by complaining is compounded. Not only are they complaining, but they do not express gratitude. They know how to talk, but only negatively; they know how to react, but only in order to grumble.

Comparing this analogy to our relationship with God leads to the following proposition: If the person who wants to complain to God for the suffering has a history of saying thank you to God for all of the good things, that person may be forgiven for lodging the complaint. However, if one never expresses gratitude for all the good that God has granted, what right does one have to complain when things go awry? Are we capable of speaking to God only when God does things we do not like? Is our faith, and our relationship with God, contingent on God's giving us exactly what we want?

This type of theology is not the Jewish way. In this regard, the Talmud states: "It is incumbent upon the individual to bless God for the bad in the same way as for the good" (*Berakhot* 54a). This speaks of the need to acknowledge God even when things are not going smoothly.

However, this is likely to happen only if an "acknowledging" relationship has already been established and one is in the habit of thanking God for the good. One who gives thanks for the good things will, upon experiencing the pain or suffering, recall all the good for which gratitude was expressed. One who daily expresses thanks for good health will, upon becoming ill, see the present travail in a different and more appreciative light.

An article in *The New York Times Magazine* (December 10, 1995, pp. 58–61) featured Mark Weiner, the star behind the puppet television show "Nickelodeon Weinerville." This article profiles Weiner and, especially, his connection to Judaism.

Weiner, whose career has experienced ups and downs, had the unfortunate experience of losing one of his children. His first-born, Avi, had a severe case of Fanconi Anemia. This is a very rare and particularly vicious disease that halts the bone marrow's production of red and white blood cells and platelets. Survival depends upon receiving a bone-marrow transplant from a matching donor.

Weiner admits that throughout this ordeal, he reversed some of his Jewishness. He uncomplicated his life by dropping religious practices one by one. "'I didn't, I still don't understand it. I don't understand how that happens'" (p. 60).

Avi died, before turning five, of a brain tumor that is associated with Fanconi Anemia. Weiner, although he has come back to some of the practices that he let go, is nevertheless not fully at peace with what befell him. "'I still believe in God,' he says. 'But my relationship with God has definitely changed. My relationship with God at this point in my life is a little . . . a little strained'" (p. 60).

Can we blame Weiner for feeling this way? Not really. I, for one, can understand what he went through, since in my lifetime I experienced the loss of a son at a very young age. There is the blessing of other children. The other children do not make up for the loss, but I cannot look upon my relationship with God as strained. If I am to be upset at God for the child that did not make it, must I not, at the same time, be absolutely delighted, happy, and appreciative to God for the children that have blossomed? We give God a bad press. Glaring tragedy we blame on God; all else we tend to take for granted. It is like air travel, the safest travel, but which scares many because of the glaring accidents that get such attention.

The "thank you" approach contains a vital concept related to recovery from illness. Rabbi Alexandri said, in the name of Rabbi Hiyya the son of Abba, that greater is the miracle that is wrought for a sick person than the miracle that occurred for Hananya, Mishael, and Azaryah. Hananya, Mishael, and Azaryah were saved from a fire that was created by a simple person, and people were able to extinguish that; however, a sick person is saved from a fire that comes from heaven, and who can extinguish that (Nedarim, 41a)?

In health and in sickness, and in recovery from illness, we are to give thanks and feel gratitude. By feeling gratitude, one relinquishes one's "ownership" of health and prosperity. Everything good is a gift; everything bad is a circumstance we must accept when it is unavoidable. There is a liberating feeling in accepting the harsh turns in life: By acceptance, one removes the bitterness. Bitterness makes the harsh situation even more unbearable; acceptance allows one to continue living in the best way possible under the circumstances.

VIII

Authentic Caring

28

The Message of Suicide

It has previously been pointed out that caring for oneself, which is a life-preserving act, is a fundamental Jewish imperative (see p. 49), and that the failure to take care of oneself is considered a serious breach (see pp. 49–54). In this regard, it is instructive to explore the issue of suicide, which goes beyond not taking care of the self. Suicide is the purposeful destroying of oneself.

The traditional Jewish attitude to suicide begins with a wholesale condemnation of the act. "One who destroys oneself wittingly has no share in the World-to-Come" is a popular Jewish saying. Interestingly, Rabbi Yekutiel Yehudah Greenwald (*Kol Bo al Avelut*, New York: Feldheim, 1965, p. 318), as well as others, point out that there is no talmudic or midrashic source for this adage; it is simply a folk saying. But the fact that the folk adopted such a saying means that this concept is undoubtedly rooted in the tradition itself.

The suicide is considered guilty of murder, albeit non-prosecutable murder, since the killer and the victim are the same person. Life is essentially a gift God has entrusted to us, but we are not allowed to exercise the rights of ownership, to destroy. We must exercise the responsibilities of trusteeship. The Talmud (*Bava Kama* 91b) interprets the words "And surely your blood of your lives will I require" (Genesis 9:5) as applying to those who spill their own blood. Both the derivation and the law are codified by Maimonides (*Mishnah Torah*, Laws of the Murderer and Guarding One's Body 2:3).

In some respects, the suicide is considered an even worse sinner than one who has committed homicide. The suicide leaves no room for repentance from the act; as well, death as a sentence from a legal tribunal serves as a catalyst for divine forgiveness, but the suicide has precluded this possibility. The suicide is also considered as having radically rejected the foundations of faith (Rabbi Yehiel Mikhel Tukacinsky, *Gesher HaHayyim*, Jerusalem, 1960, pp. 269–270).

Included in the category of suicide are acts of negligence that lead to one's death, such as inciting a fight that leads to being killed, or walking a dangerous path—for instance, walking on thin ice over a body of water and then falling through the ice (Judah the Pious, *Sefer Hasidim*, Jerusalem: Mossad HaRav Kook, 1970, para. 675). These actions are suicidal in outcome, if not in intent. One must answer for negligence, since in negligence one has failed to maintain watchfulness over life, thereby failing to affirm the sanctity of life.

The Rabbis have forbidden many actions because of their potential danger to life. Failure to adhere to these prohibitions makes one subject to the punishment of "flogging for rebelling" (Maimonides, *Mishnah Torah*, Laws of the Murderer and Guarding One's Body 11:5). The Rabbis, it may be said, tried to prevent even the passive suicide.

The far-reaching scope of the suicide prohibition, as applied by the Rabbis, is a further indication of the seriousness with which Judaism regards the preservation of life. Further study of the laws concerning suicide, however, reveals a most illuminating post facto sensitivity, with great implications for broader issues concerning life and death.

The suicide is denied the normal rights of burial.

> We do not occupy ourselves in any respect with funeral rights of one who committed suicide willfully .... We do not rend garments for him, bare the shoulder, or deliver a memorial address over him. We do, however, stand in a row for him and recite the benediction of mourners for him, from respect of the living [relatives]. The general rule is: With anything that makes for respect of the living we occupy ourselves, but with anything that does not make for respect of the living, the public does not in any way occupy itself (*Semahot* 2:1).

The suicide is separated from the burial ceremony. Attention is focused on the needs of the surviving family. No disrespect is shown for the suicide, in deference to the living; any respect shown for the suicide is for the sake of living.

What is said at the burial of a suicide? There is a difference of opinion. Rabbi Yishmael's view is that we exclaim over the suicide: "Alas for a lost [life]! Alas for [lost] life!" Rabbi Akiva disagrees, stating that we should leave the suicide unmourned: "Speak neither well nor ill of him" (*Semahot* 2:1).

Rabbi Yishmael's view, one may surmise, involves consistency: If Jewish tradition condemns suicide, it ought to be lamented at burial, in order to affirm tradition and, it is hoped, to prevent further suicides. Rabbi Akiva finds that silence is the best approach, either out of deference to the surviving family, or out of consideration for the suicide; perhaps there may be extenuating circumstances that make blame inappropriate. Within these differing opinions one finds the roots of the developing and, indeed, complex Judaic attitude toward suicide—an attitude that incorporates, at once, condemnation and understanding.

The term the Talmud and later authorities employ to describe suicide is "destroying oneself wittingly" (*me'abed atzmo lada'at*). This terminology relates to two aspects of suicide: the act (destroying) and the intent. Excluded from this are the legitimate martyr (who affirms rather than destroys life) and one who is not fully in control of one's wits at the time of suicide.

The basic rule of suicide is expressed in the Talmud.

> Who [comes within the category of] "one who committed suicide willfully"? One does not who climbed to the top of a tree and fell down and died, or one who went up to the top of the roof and fell down and died. But one who calls out, "Look, I am going to the top of the roof or to the top of the tree, and I will throw myself down that I may die" [comes within the category]. When the people saw him go up to the top of a tree or roof [for the purpose] and he fell down and died, he is presumed to have committed suicide willfully (*Semahot* 2:2).

To satisfy the conditions for suicide, one must announce the intention to commit suicide and then carry out that expressed intention in the view of others. An intervening period of substantial duration between the expression and the act disqualifies the act as suicide; it is presumed that the suicide had a change of heart in the interim.

As is the case with capital crimes, with suicide there is, in Jewish law, a presumption of innocence. "If a person was found strangled, or hanging from a tree, or lying dead on a sword, he is presumed not to have committed suicide willfully, and none [of the rights] are withheld from him" (*Semahot* 2:3). A more contemporary authority applies this ruling even to a case in which it is evident that the act was perpetrated by the victim, and homicide is ruled out. It may be suicide, but it is assumed to have occurred without the victim's full wits; the victim was overcome by an evil spirit (insanity, perhaps) or a fear-evoking circumstance (Hatam Sofer, *Yoreh De'ah*, responsa 326).

Tukacinsky (*Gesher HaHayyim*, pp. 271–273) spells out the conditions that must exist for a person to be condemned as a suicide, and to be denied the rights of religious burial. Even if one announces the intention to shoot oneself and is later found shot, the announced intention is not connected to the act. We assume that people exaggerate and do not always mean what they say. Only if the victim followed the intention with immediate action is such a case eligible to be labeled suicide. Even if one left a note, it cannot be assumed that there is a direct connection between the suicide note and the act.

Tukacinsky quotes other authorities who rule out certain forms of killing the self as suicide. Even a drowning that immediately follows an expressed intention to do so cannot be considered suicide; drowning takes a while, in which time one wrestles with the agony of dying. It is assumed that in the few moments prior to death one repented from the act of killing oneself (*Gesher HaHayyim*, p. 272). This exemption applies to any form of suicide in which there is an intervening period of consciousness between the act and death.

This liberal attitude is not inconsistent with the previously mentioned prohibition against any form of self-damage. Every individual is answerable for the inflicting of damage on oneself, but not every self-inflicted death qualifies as suicide, with all the attendant restrictions imposed upon the suicide. Answerability is an other-worldly concept; it is in God's hands. Suicide is a this-worldly judgment made by people about others' actions.

> The law of destroying oneself is only conceivable in a situation wherein the victim himself established with absolute certainty that he killed himself with a clear mind, and without an intervening period for regret (Tukacinsky, *Gesher HaHayyim*, p. 272).

Clear intent and the guarantee that this intent was never compromised are requisites for labeling an act as suicide. Tukacinsky cites a view that a person who kills himself or herself because of a multitude of troubles and worries is not considered a suicide. This is a very liberal interpretation of the term "clear mind," and it removes the worried person from having killed himself or herself "wittingly."

Others add another proviso to legitimize the suicide label. The suicide must previously have been forewarned by two witnesses that the act is criminal and of capital import, and the suicide must have accepted this warning. This precaution is applied in most cases of capital crimes. Tukacinsky mentions the sources for this view and considers this view strong enough to be relied upon when there is other supporting evidence mitigating the circumstances.

Forewarning is another way of establishing that the suicide was in full possession of his or her wits when committing the act. The witnesses who forewarned the suicide must testify that the victim was of a clear enough mind to fully absorb the message.

Thus, although Judaism wholly condemns the act of suicide, the person involved is not so readily condemned. In the view of Rabbi Y.M. Epstein, we look for the slightest possibility of doubt to avoid branding an individual as a suicide (*Arukh HaShulhan*, Yoreh De'ah 345:5). Tukacinsky agrees with this view and adopts this stance as normative, but he rejects the view that excludes one overcome by trouble and worries from being considered a suicide. If that were the case, says Tukacinsky, "there would be no instance of destroying oneself, because anyone who destroys the self does so because of pain" (*Gesher HaHayyim*, p. 273).

Tukacinsky would like the theoretical stance toward suicide to have some factual basis; if no actual suicide is possible, then there is no concept of suicide that is rooted in reality. Greenwald points out, however, that the Sages searched so many times "for excuses and positive points about the one who destroyed the self wittingly, until there is not to be found, in truth, a case of one who destroyed the self wittingly" (*Kol Bo al Avelut*, p. 319).

There is a danger in stating that Judaism condemns suicide unconditionally. This view fails to take into account Judaism's humane stance toward the killer–victim and the hesitancy even to employ the label of suicide, or to apply the legal decree associated with suicide.

This approach, eminently humane and psychologically perceptive as it is, nevertheless seems inconsistent. However, before examining the consistency or inconsistency of this approach, it should be noted that there is a great similarity between this approach and the general attitude to affliction and the causes thereof.

The fact that affliction is often associated with wrongs we may have committed in no way reflects a condemnation of the individual. Consider the fact that the suicide, who perpetrates a serious crime, is not condemned after the fact. Jewish tradition evidences a great sensitivity for the individual in any and all circumstances. To suggest, therefore, that because suffering is associated with human deficiency this is a disparaging judgment on the human being is completely unwarranted.

In the instances of suicide reported in the Talmud, including that of the fuller (*Ketuvot* 103b) and Rabbi Hiyya bar Abba (*Kiddushin* 81b), for example, we find no condemnation of these individuals after the fact. If these individuals had asked in advance whether their actions were legitimate, the answer would have been an absolute no; once the action had already been taken, however, we find a different mindset. The same is true of the reaction to the attempted suicide of King Saul (Midrash Rabbah, Genesis 34:13; see also *Shulhan Arukh*, Yoreh De'ah 345:3).

In addition, the martyr—who though acting with full wits, is not acting destructively but, rather, in a constructive manner—not only is not consid-

ered a suicide, but also is lauded for the heroic behavior associated with martyrdom.

The trend within Jewish tradition is quite clear:
Suicide is condemned before the fact, but after the
fact there is a dramatic shift and change of view.
Why is it that suicide, so condemned in theory, is
virtually eliminated in fact?

Suicide is usually prompted by a situation in
which the individual sees no future for himself or
herself. Suicide is not a leap into the afterlife; it is,
rather, an escape from this world. Judaism cautions
against such escapism: "And let not your evil in-
clination assure you that the grave is a place of
refuge for you" (*Avot* 4:22). From the theological
perspective, there is no escape.

The underlying common denominator in the
Judaic attitude to suicide is the unconditional affirmation of the meaningfulness of life. Within this
context there are two views: the prospective view
and the retrospective view. Prospectively, there is
a confidence that life will afford the opportunity
for fulfillment and that no situation legitimizes
taking away what God has given. The Rabbis tried
to eliminate the possibility of suicide by condemn-
ing it as legally forbidden and as morally and theologically reprehensible, consistent with scriptural
statements to that effect.

Retrospectively, for those who had already
committed suicide, the Rabbis had an abundance
of sympathy and understanding. In their affirmative stance toward life, they valiantly tried to see
the affirmative in the suicide act, or at least to see
mitigating circumstances that would excuse the act

as not being the normal expression of the killer–victim.

There is such a confidence about life that the Rabbis refuse to believe that, in normal circumstances, one would take one's life. If this happened, it was obviously an abnormal expression brought on by inner turmoil or external pressure. The Rabbis walk a thin line, but by doing so they combine theological doctrine and psychological insight, fusing them into a humane and understanding approach. It is an approach that seeks to affirm life both before and after, and is profoundly instructive to the theme of suffering and affliction.

29

The Rationale for the Rationale

The concern for infusing life and death—even death by suicide—with meaning must also, therefore, pervade the rabbinic understanding of suffering.

The fact is that in almost all the rabbinic writings concerning suffering, the theme of suffering, as it relates to personal failings, constantly surfaces. This view is too widespread to dismiss as merely the opinion of one individual; in every generation, and amongst the greatest of the Sages, this approach to suffering is the standard. That being so, the question that comes to mind is: Why is this the case?

The simple answer is that the Sages expressed themselves in this way because it is the unavoidable, inescapable truth that personal failings are connected to suffering. However, the fact that this is continually expressed causes us to pause and ask what is the implication of the constant repetition of this theme.

To suggest that this shows an insensitivity to the human being is certainly outlandish. From the sensitive way in which the Rabbis handle the issue of suicide, it is apparent that the Rabbis were empathetic individuals who cared deeply about life and about people, and who cared deeply about infusing life with purpose.

One thing is clear from this general appreciation of rabbinic sensitivity: When the Rabbis continually drummed home the connection between wrongdoing and affliction, their repetition was not made as a put-down of the person so afflicted. The fact that the Sages voiced the understanding that affliction is very often an expression of God's love and concern, that God would not do this to someone whom God did not care about, and that the affliction is imposed for beneficial reasons, further drives home this point.

It would be difficult to accept any other proposition. We cannot accept the notion that suffering comes undeservedly; we certainly cannot accept the proposition that God causes us agony and pain for no reason. As a matter of fact, to believe this is sacrilege.

The consequences of deservedness may pose a psychological challenge, but it is a challenge that can be easily overcome. If it is a psychological challenge that stems from the presumption that "if God is punishing me, I must be bad," that is patently wrong. It is clear from the sources that the opposite is true.

We cannot countenance the view that God has nothing to do with all this. If we are to believe certain self-appointed theologians of this generation who claim that God has nothing to do with what has transpired and that these tragedies just "happened," then we will have gone beyond compromising our understanding of God. We will also have severely curtailed our ability to take responsibility for our failings, and to do our best to rise above them.

The Rabbis were confident that, in the long run, telling people that their suffering resulted from their own behavior would not be taken as a denial of their sense of self-worth. On the contrary, this can be seen in a more enlightened perspective as giving individuals a sense of *empowerment*, that it is in their hands to make their situation better; if not better in this world, at least in the ultimate reality of *olam haba*. Viktor Frankl's reference to the remark of Max Scheler comes to mind: "Man has a *right* to be considered guilty and to be punished. Once we deal with man as the victim of circumstances and their influences, we not only cease to treat him as a human being but also *lame* his will to change" (Viktor Frankl, *The Will to Meaning: Foundations and Applications of Logotherapy*, New York: World Publishing Co., 1969, p. 74).

What Jewish tradition, as expressed in Scripture and in rabbinic writings, offers concerning illness and suffering is undoubtedly bitter medicine; it is much easier to say that all this has nothing to do with us; it just "happened." But, as bitter a pill as it is, it is also a helpful medicine. Despite the possible danger of misinterpreting their view as an assault on one's sense of self, the Rabbis drummed home their message—aware of the risks, but confident of the final results.

The Sages refused to believe that we live in a world that happened by chance, or in which the most serious occurrences in life happened by chance. As challenging as this may be in terms of our understanding of why God has brought affliction upon us, it is preferable to a world in which God is absent. In other words, it is rabbinic confidence in our ability to continually improve ourselves and to have the strength and the courage to rise above painful circumstance that is at work in this approach.

In the Rabbis' stance, there is no attempt to protect God from wrongful accusation by saying that what happened was really an accident, or was done by others and that God had nothing to do with it. The Rabbis confronted the issue head-on, aware of the risks, but aware as well that a theologically fraudulent approach, though comforting in the short run, for the moment, would be more devastating in the long run.

30

Guilt and Empowerment

The history of the Jewish people begins with the first professed monotheist, the Patriarch Abraham. Abraham's descendants, ostensibly through no fault of their own, were thrust into exile for a protracted period.

The Talmud (*Nedarim* 32a) gives a few explanations of why Abraham's children were punished for Abraham's wrongs by their descent into enslavement in Egypt. Among the reasons offered is that Abraham pressed God too much about God's ways; he asked for the means to verify the covenantal promise.

It makes little sense that for this Abraham's children had to suffer. Why the children? And what was so objectionable in Abraham's request? Maharal (loc. cit.) explains that Abraham was not fully strengthened in faith; therefore God sent his de-

scendants into exile, so that they could acquire faith
and experience God's power and strength.

As to why the children and not Abraham himself had to bear this affliction, Maharal states that a
deficiency in the root of a tree is more obvious in
the branches than in the root itself. The branches—
the children of Israel—rather than the root—Abraham—suffered in order to grow.

The early history of the Israelites is a history
of suffering and a lesson about suffering. No guilt
or sin was involved in this collective agony, but
there was a need to entrench spiritual values—faith
and hope, empathy and caring. Guilt, no; suffering, yes. This can occur on a personal level or on
a communal level.

On a national level, the destruction of the two
Holy Sanctuaries, and the subsequent thrusting of
the Jewish people into exile, was, and still is, considered a great calamity. We know that the destruction of the First Holy Sanctuary was perpetrated
by the Babylonians and that of the Second Holy
Sanctuary by the Romans. Nevertheless, on every
festival, we recite a statement that "it was because
of our sins that we were exiled from our land . . . ."
How do we reconcile history with this statement?
How can we say that we were exiled because of
our sins when, in fact, we were exiled because we
were beaten by superior fire-power?

There is ample explanation to justify this statement on purely historical grounds. At the time of
the second destruction, for example, the Jewish
people were bitterly divided, to the point that
internecine bickering between the factions led to

the destruction of supplies in Jerusalem that would have enabled the population to successfully resist the siege (*Gittin* 55b–56a).

Because of the destruction of these supplies, which was done not by an external enemy but by internal forces, a capitulation was forced that perhaps could have been avoided altogether. Purely on those grounds, one may simply state that we had the ability to resist and, possibly, even to overcome, but our resistance fell far short of the mark because we did not have a sense of community. There was too much mutual enmity, enmity that is totally alien—or, at least, ought to be alien—to Jewish tradition.

Parenthetically, it should be noted that Jewish tradition views being sent into exile as an act of compassion for us on God's part (*Pesahim* 87b). By our being spread out, it is difficult for Israel's enemies to utterly destroy us. Also, our living among other peoples causes Jewish values to be witnessed by example, thereby inspiring others to emulate them.

However, there are other dimensions to the comment that we were exiled because of our sins. Simply put, if it is because of our sins that we were exiled, then it stands to reason that if those sins are corrected, the exile will come to an end. In other words, by stating that we are to blame for our fate, we are given a sense of *empowerment*.

All too often, we take blame as a crushing blow to our individual or collective self-esteem. But this is not the intention, and it should not be interpreted as such. We are simply being told that the ball is in

our court, for better and for worse. It is our obligation to make the best of our circumstances.

Were the exile to have been explained away
as an inexorable progression of history, with certain forces overpowering other forces slightly less
powerful, then there really would have been no
hope. How could a nation completely destroyed
by a more powerful nation ever entertain even a
legitimate hope of regaining its home and its sanctuary? It would have been a very remote hope, and
one would have been ridiculed as being wholly
unrealistic.

The Sages knew this, and realized that any as-
piration for return must be grounded in terms
other than an historical analysis of power posi-
tions. The Sages told the people that had they been
on the right level spiritually, they could have re-
sisted more powerful forces; that their own spiritual weakness made them vulnerable to these
forces. However, the Sages also gave the people a
powerful, enduring message of hope: that if they
did unite spiritually and communally, then they
would be able to return. It was not hopeless and
never will be, because redemption is in our own
hands.

Moving from the communal to the personal,
therefore, if we are told that our suffering is because
of our sins, we should not take this as a blow to our
self-esteem; on the contrary, we should see this as
an affirmation of our own power to correct our circumstance, and an uncompromising affirmation
of the esteem in which we are held. This does not
mean that, in all instances, repentance will elimi-

nate the cancer, or that soul-searching will correct the heart failure. If it were that easy, even the atheist would embrace this medical formula.

Such a system of automatic cure would be an intrusion on the notion of free choice for the good that the person opts to affirm not because of what is gained materially, but simply because it is correct. Repentance as a means for regaining pure physical health would reduce this spiritual affirmation to a tool for material gain, and would rob repentance of its intrinsic meaning. Repentance, rather than being an end in itself, would become a means to another end.

Yes, empowerment is implied in the statement that there is no suffering without sin. But the ultimate recompense involved in the process of soul-searching as a result of affliction is not immediately apparent; it is more a promise of a "spiritual balance of payments" in some future realm, referred to as *olam haba*. Since *olam haba* is a reality that is dependent on faith, then the pureness of the choice of repentance is maintained. We do not repent because of reward; the reality of ultimate reward sharpens our focus on ultimate values.

At the same time, the fair and, therefore, necessary notion that goodness does not go unrewarded, whether here or in the future, is likewise maintained. It is a delicate balance, but it is a balance that touches on all the important issues in a fair and equitable way, with all the exceptions that cause the vexing problems.

This sense of empowerment, and its concomitant opening up of possibilities for meaning, is profoundly illustrated in God's reaction after Israel surrendered to the lure of idolatry. God said to Moses: "Leave me alone so that I may destroy them" (Exodus 32:10). When Moses heard this, he immediately jumped into the fray with vigor, saying that if God said to leave God alone, this meant that he had something to do with it, and that he could do something about it (Exodus 32:10, and Rashi, loc. cit.; *Midrash Tanhuma*, Ki Tissa 22).

Moses did, indeed, forcefully argue against God's desire to destroy Israel (*Berakhot* 32a–b). And the intervention of Moses was perfectly consistent with the same type of intervention undertaken by Abraham upon his hearing about God's intentions concerning the city of Sodom. Is it sacrilegious to suggest that God actually wants us to react in this way, that God spurs us to action by conferring upon us a dose of suffering and affliction?

The Rabbis knew what they doing when they established a sense of balance regarding suicide. And they knew what they were doing when they incessantly emphasized the connection between affliction and our own behavior. Their approach, seemingly harsh, is rooted in a profound and ultimate sensitivity, rather than in a fleeting feel-good type of theology that may serve well for the moment but actually is counterproductive and possibly even destructive.

We all make mistakes, often serious ones. These mistakes need not define who we are; they must only inspire us to become better.

IX

BIKUR HOLIM

31

The Visitor's Importance

A person who is ill and facing the dark reality of life's termination very often feels lonely. This is especially so when the ill person contemplates the fullness of life in the immediate surroundings and the reality that he or she will not be part of that life in a very short period of time. There is a strong and piercing feeling of being cut off from the vibrancy of this world.

Added to this is the unfortunate reality that many people withdraw from those who are not well. It is as if the person diagnosed with cancer or another terminal illness has suddenly become a pariah who has been inflicted with a terrible plague and must be avoided. No matter how many times people are told that it is important to visit the sick, they still avoid visiting the afflicted individual.

Often, simply the fear of being unable to handle the situation or not knowing what to say to the patient keeps people away. This is unfortunate, especially when the failure to offer support, to voice one's concerns and express one's best wishes, can destroy what heretofore had been a reasonably sound friendship. The purist might argue that if the friendship were sound this would not happen, but this is difficult to prove.

One of the most effective, strength-giving experiences for a person in the throes of illness is a visit by someone who has had a similar experience, who is living and is able to tell the tale. Understandably, not all illnesses have happy endings, and not all circumstances lend themselves to such an approach. When viable, however, a visit by someone who has had a similar diagnosis, is fighting it vigorously, and is able to maintain some form of functionality in the midst of treatment is often a source of inspiration. Support groups composed of many such individuals are, likewise, immensely helpful.

Sometimes, whether we like it or not, people relate better to strangers than they do to their most intimate family and friends. This is not to say that it is good, but it is a reality. It is important to be cognizant of this in terms of mapping out strategies that can be helpful to the person in the throes of the illness.

32

A Unique *Mitzvah*

Visiting people who are ill is one of the most important precepts within the general category of concern for other individuals. Indeed, the obligation to visit the sick is one of the vast array of *mitzvot* (precepts) aimed at easing the plight of individuals in unfortunate circumstances. These precepts include the obligation to be sensitive to the situation of the widow and the orphan, the obligation to support those who have fallen upon hard times, and so on.

Bikur holim, the obligation to visit the sick, is a sacred obligation. Although it is certainly consistent with the full complement of obligations previously mentioned, it more precisely falls within the scope of that famous, all-encompassing commandment, to *love your neighbor as yourself* (Leviticus 19:18).

We are obliged to do for our neighbors what we would want them to do for us in similar circumstances. Certainly most people, when they become ill, welcome visits from others, especially if the visits will cheer them, inspire them, infuse them with a sense of purpose, and invigorate them with more resolve to fight the disease. If that is what the sick person would like, then surely it behooves us to visit. Obviously, we should first make sure that this is the ailing person's desire, but, lacking information, it is preferable to visit rather than to refrain from doing so.

It is Maimonides (*Laws of Mourning* 14:1) who suggests that visiting the sick is in the category of "Love your neighbor as yourself" (Leviticus 19:18). On the other hand, *Sefer Haredim* states that the obligation to visit the sick comes from a different, more primary source. Maimonides' view is that the obligation to visit is rabbinic in nature, but is a fulfillment of a general biblical principle. According to *Sefer Haredim*, when the Torah states "And you shall make known to them the way in which they should go . . ." (Exodus 18:20), it is referring to visiting the sick. One way to fulfill this precept is by talking with the sick person, because talk is beneficial to that person (*Sefer Haredim*, Affirmative Commandments of Biblical Origin That Relate to Speech and Can Be Fulfilled Daily 12:47).

Regarding the verse, "You shall follow the ways of God" (Deuteronomy 13:5), the Talmud (*Sotah* 14a) interprets this to mean that one should emulate God's ways. Just as God visits the sick, so, too, are we obliged to visit the sick. *Bikur holim* is accorded a transcending, Godly importance.

Bikur holim is traditionally translated to mean visiting the sick; however, there is a more revealing nuance to this term. The word *bikur* (visiting) is related to the word for morning, or *boker*. When we visit the sick, we are, in effect, charged with the responsibility of showing them the "morning," or bright side, of life.

One who is unwell is understandably verging on melancholy, depression, or despondency at the unwelcome circumstance. For that person the world is black, the sun is setting, and there is no light. By visiting, and, it is to be hoped, bringing a renewed spirit to the sick person, we remove that despondency, we remove the darkness, and instead infuse the individual with a "daytime," or *boker*, feeling.

So, *Bikur holim* is the obligation to, among other things, bring brightness and sunshine and hope—yes, that all-important word, hope—into the lives of those individuals who are not well. The very terminology of the *mitzvah* speaks profoundly about what it is all about.

The effect that a visit to the sick has, aside from the obvious, relates to a lovely midrashic equation (*Midrash Rabbah*, Numbers 16:10). One lifting a weight on one's own can lift just so much, but if one lifts this weight together with a friend, then they can lift triple the amount. In other words, when people gather together to support each other, they can do much more than individuals can achieve on their own. This is one of the most vital components of the obligation to visit the sick.

The Talmud states that there is no limit to visiting the sick. What does this mean? In the view of Abaye, this means that a greater individual should visit a lesser individual; in other words, a person of great importance in the community should visit the ordinary citizens. Rava adds that it means even a hundred times in the course of a day. Obviously, this is only if such is necessary, and is not a burden to the ill person (*Nedarim* 39b; see also *Shulhan Arukh*, Yoreh De'ah 335:2).

Anyone who is able to plead for mercy for a friend and fails to do so is considered a sinner (*Berakhot* 12b). Interestingly, one of the major components of visiting the sick is the entreaty to God, following the visit, to grant recovery to the sick person (*Shulhan Arukh*, Yoreh De'ah 335:4). Without such entreaty, one has not fulfilled the precept concerning visiting the sick. We must care not only socially, but spiritually.

We must be especially careful with our words when visiting. When visiting the sick, or one who is suffering a trauma, such as the loss of a child, one should not speak in the manner that Job's friends spoke to him, suggesting that no one is visited with suffering who is clear of sin (*Bava Mezia* 58b). This is in the category of verbal affliction, and is prohibited (Deuteronomy 25:17).

There is another side to this sacred obligation. The failure to visit an afflicted person is a serious breach. Maharal, in his commentary to *Nedarim*

40a, states that visiting brings a contented spirit to the sick person, and that the visit in itself is, therefore, potentially salvational.

Maharal expounds on this *mitzvah* with his usual eloquence. Combining the rational and the mystical, he states that the ill person can reach all the way to the gates of death, and yet it is still possible for others to help the person. This can be achieved through a simple deed that will help the sick person; for example, by making the person feel better with a visit, or by praying to God on the person's behalf. One who is able to do so but fails to is considered as if he had spilled blood, in the view of Rabbi Akiva (*Nedarim* 40a). Rabbi Akiva taught that suffering is precious, but that failing to ease the suffering of others is sinful.

Thus we have a collective responsibility to visit those who will benefit from the visit. And, as the Talmud states, an important person's visiting someone of lesser importance does have a great impact. We often read about sports heroes who give a great lift to adoring fans who are sick by visiting them in the hospital. There are lovely stories of hospital patients who are visited by the President or Prime Minister of their country. The sick person is uplifted by the sense of importance engendered by the esteemed visitor.

The visit of a close friend also raises the spirits of a sick person, not so much from the honor of making a visit, but from the obvious emotional impact the visit has. To a good friend one can pour out one's soul; one can ask for certain small favors that one may be reluctant to ask of others.

These little things can make a big difference—the difference between life and death, between hope and despair.

One of the nicest things a friend can do for one who is ill is to be a catalyst for the ailing person's spiritual recovery. It is a *mitzvah* to help the sick person to repent, to look inward, to search the soul (*Sefer Haredim*, Biblical Affirmative Commands That Are Related to Speech and That Can Be Fulfilled Every Day 4:48). However, that can be done only by a very close friend, and, even then, only with the utmost delicacy.

Ultimately, the main task of visiting is to help. Ours is not to judge, or to impose a rationale for the illness on the suffering patient. We dare not justify the pain; we must dare to alleviate it.

X

BEING CLOSE

33

The Physician

As important as it is for the patient to choose a good physician, it is wrong for any patient to believe that the healing process is strictly in the physician's hands. I cringe when I hear people say that they have "faith" in their doctor. One may have confidence in one's doctor, but faith is reserved for God.

The equation most conducive to optimizing the possibility of cure includes a patient with faith in God, confidence in the physician, and firm resolve to fight the illness at all levels. To this tripartite approach to illness must be added the all-important ingredient of support from family and friends.

The role of the physician in the healing process, as well as the function of other ingredients of the healing process, are nicely presented in *Ecclesiasticus*, by Ben Sira.

First, the best medicine is preventive. We must take care of ourselves so that we do not need the physician. "Honor the physician before need of the physician, for the physician too has God endowed" (*Ecclesiasticus* 38:1).

In the area of prevention, spiritual matters are of critical importance. "Flee from sin and from obsequiousness, and from all iniquity cleanse your heart" (*Ecclesiasticus* 38:10).

We must respect the physician. "And also to the physician give due, and do not relent for also in the physician is there need" (*Ecclesiasticus* 38:12).

A good physician gains the blessing of healing from God. Not only the physician, but also the patient, must realize this. "There is a time when in (the doctor's) hand is success, for the doctor too will pray to God, that God prosper unto the doctor the treatment and the healing, for the sake of the living" (*Ecclesiasticus* 38:13).

The patient must take an active role in the healing process, rather than simply relying on medical intervention. This involves addressing the spiritual component of the illness. "My child, in sickness be not negligent; pray unto God for God will heal" (*Ecclesiasticus* 38:9).

Medicines are a Godly gift toward health; we should not hesitate to make use of them. "God brings forth medicines from the earth; let the prudent person not reject them" (*Ecclesiasticus* 38:4).

A friend of mine recently shared with me an interesting story. His brother, an investment broker, has many people who depend upon his advice on investment strategies. During a particularly trying time, the market barometers were going south, and many people were worried about what to do with their money. Many people asked this investment broker what to do, and he responded to all of them. After the crisis abated, he told his brother that of all the people who had asked him what do do, only he, his brother, had asked the right question. My friend was perplexed, since he did not recall asking a question. But the investment-broker brother reminded him that while everyone else asked what they should do with their money, he had asked, "What are *you* doing with *your* money?"

This small episode illustrates the type of approach one should take when being cared for by a physician. Problems can arise in deciding which therapy to embark upon—surgery versus chemotherapy or radiation, for example, or pills versus surgery for heart difficulties. The variations are endless. It is a good idea, when approaching the physician, to ask not what you should do, but what the physician would do if it was his or her life that was involved. This does not mean that you must do what the doctor would do, but you will get a much more accurate picture of the options and an idea as to the most viable of the available strategies.

The physician should never deny a patient the capacity to hope. Even if the person is leaning toward death, the doctor should not say: "Go and give your final testaments to the household." To do this would be wrong, because the physician should not cause the patient to give up on recovery (*Kohelet Rabbah* 5:4).

On the patient's side, since physicians have many things to do, it is best not to be a nag, asking unnecessary questions and bothering doctors needlessly. On the other hand, the physician should expect that since the patient's life is at stake, the patient will want to ask many questions. The doctor may have heard these questions many times, and may become impatient upon hearing them once again.

The physician must remember that even though a thousand patients may ask the same question, each patient is asking it for the first time. The question must be treated with patience each time the physician hears it. That beautiful instruction about being patient in judgment, which is addressed to judges in a specific case (*Avot* 1:1), applies also to the practice of medicine.

Doctors make serious judgments, judgments often much more serious than those made by a judge. The judge must not look upon a case that seems similar to another case and make a snap decision based on what was heard previously; instead, the judge is adjured to "be patient in rendering judgment," to handle each situation as if it were a first-time case. The physician, similarly, must look upon each patient in this way and judge each case with patience, deliberation, and an appreciation of the sanctity of life and its importance to the person wrestling with the illness.

Showing patience means that although doctors may sometimes be in a hurry because they are overloaded with responsibilities, nevertheless it is wrong for them to rush the patient away.

At some time in the physician–patient relationship, preferably at an early stage, the physician should set aside some time—not necessarily a long time—to sit down with the patient and hear the patient out. The patient will be left feeling that the physician really cares, that the doctor is taking the time to listen attentively. After this occurs, everything flows much more smoothly. This is the "long way" that actually works out to be the short way (*Eruvin* 52b). The doctor will thereby be a better doctor, and the patient will be happier and more relaxed.

Too often, doctors don't take the time to speak to their patients, thereby frustrating and angering them and causing a deterioration in the patient's emotional state and perhaps even the physical condition. This downward spiral in the physician–patient relationship also affects the physician's relationship with the rest of the family. Communication at the very outset establishes a firm and understanding relationship, so that later on, when the physician actually is in a hurry, the patient will understand.

Why is it that some patients say that their doctor is always too busy to talk, and others say that their doctor is busy but always has time for them?

In some instances, the reason is the "*kvetch*" factor:
Some patients always complain, and others are always appreciative. In other cases, though, it is the
doctor factor. If the doctor establishes a caring relationship at the outset, then everything afterwards
is icing on the cake; but if the doctor never takes
the time, then each hurried visit builds negativity
upon negativity.

The physician's obligation to engage in healing is more than an obligation to apply medical
knowledge. It is also an obligation to apply human
feeling, because that, too, is life-enhancing, and is
an integral ingredient of the healing process. For
a patient to have confidence in the doctor means
confidence in not only the doctor's technical abilities, but also the doctor's human sensitivities.

If the physician is to exercise the biblical obligation to engage in healing, then certainly the
physician must demonstrate humane concern and
take the time to understand the patient. The patient is not just simply someone with an illness;
the patient is a human being with many thoughts,
anxieties, and worries. These concerns must be
fully appreciated if the physician is to be a complete physician.

If a person has an anxiety, let that person
relate that anxiety to a friend (*Yoma* 75a). Life-
threatening illness is bound to generate a high
level of anxiety, and the physician is uniquely
equipped to address this anxiety as a friend. By
being a true friend, the physician becomes a true
healer.

34

The Family

The issue of a child's care of an ill or infirm parent is a sensitive one. And the problems related to this are not one-sided.

Some parents would very much like their children to devote a great deal of time and attention to them. These parents are much better served if they do not make demands on their children. As Rabbi Eliezer Papo remarks, if parents see that the children do not have the desire to help, they should not impose upon them; but if they see that the children are eager, then it is a *mitzvah* to afford them the opportunity to behave meritoriously (*Pele Yoetz*, 265–266). That way, the children do what they can not because they are forced to do so, but because they actually want to do so. If the parent pressures the child, the child will build up a well of resentment.

As always, within the realm of possibility, it is best to have a frank discussion of parental expectations and filial ability to accommodate these expectations. The parent may want to have the child's constant care, but the child may not be able to provide it. The child who tells the parent that he or she would very much like to do this, but—for reasons that are fully understandable, including family responsibility—simply cannot, may alleviate some of the pressures or unspoken demands that the parent may have but the child simply cannot meet.

Openness about the issues is essential, even though this may be harder to achieve than it sounds. If the child has been neglectful in the past and the parent now truly needs the child, this is an opportunity for the child to go beyond self-justification and admit to being less appreciative a child than he or she should have been. This works much better than if the parent tells the child this. The talmudic phrase that a little bit of self-flagellation is more effective than a hundred lashes (*Berakhot* 7a) speaks directly to this.

It is much better for individuals to acknowledge on their own where they have gone wrong and to try to improve their behavior than to be told by others where they have gone wrong. In the normal pattern of human relations, when people are told where they have gone wrong, immediately they get defensive, and they will deny it or do other things to protect their dignity. As irrational as this may be, it is nevertheless a predictable reaction.

So, in the situation of illness, it is so much more appropriate for the people directly affected by the family member's illness to do some serious soul-searching and then grow into much better people than they had been previously. Good will, a sincere desire to help, foregoing of ego concerns, ignoring old agendas or past hurts: All are necessary qualities that help to strengthen and support the family relationship.

In the parent–child interaction, one of the primary difficulties is not necessarily the reluctance of children to help their parents (which does happen); just as serious is the reluctance of parents to accept their children's help. This is somewhat understandable, given that for a long time the parents were the givers rather than the receivers of the help. It can be an upsetting and difficult change for the parent.

Parents, however, should take seriously the direct obligation that children are given: "Honor your father and your mother" (Exodus 20:12). The Talmud (*Kiddushin* 31b) is very clear about how to fulfill this obligation. We do this by feeding our parents, dressing them, escorting them out, and bringing them home. Why is this how we are to honor our parents, when, in reality, it is the parent who dresses the child, feeds the child, takes the child out, and brings the child home until the child has become independent enough to do these things?

This talmudic dictum addresses the time in life when the roles are reversed—when the child is an adult, but the parent has deteriorated and is suffering through the degenerative patterns of old age. Precisely at this juncture, when the parent now becomes childlike in behavior and the child is more adult in behavior, the adult child is asked to repay the parent and do for the parent at that time what the parent had done for the child in the child's earlier stages of life. This is simply the repayment of a tangible debt, whereby the child avoids being considered a repudiator of the good that has been done for him or her, a character deficiency that is considered quite serious in Jewish thought (*Sefer Haredim*, Affirmative Commands of Kabbalah Origin and from the Soferim That Are Contingent on the Heart and Can Be Fulfilled Daily 1:23).

Since the child is obliged to care for the parent when the roles are reversed, it is important for parents to learn to accept this. This means that when the time comes that they need care and the child offers to provide such care, the parent must graciously allow this. Parents must be aware that by refusing to accept help, they are making it difficult for the children to fulfill their biblical obligation. And no parent would want to do that to a child.

35

The Pain of the Spouse

There is a famous talmudic stricture prohibiting a couple from engaging in conjugal union in the daylight hours, or from staring at one's spouse (*Nedarim* 20a; *Niddah* 16b–17a). The primary message of both of these strictures is obviously not to curtail the sensual pleasure of the conjugal union. Such pleasure is considered an exalted and noble part of the marital discourse, and even is referred to as the holy of holies (*The Holy Letter*, attributed to Nahmanides, Chaps. 2 & 5; see also Reuven P. Bulka, *Jewish Marriage: An Halakhic Ethic*, New York and Hoboken: Ktav Publishing House and Yeshiva University Press, 1986, Chap. 10).

Rather, this is intended to impress, most specifically the husband, that one's spouse is not a object, but is rather a human being. One loves not what the other person has, but what the other person is. When the body becomes wrinkled later in life, or when the ravages of illness intrude upon one's looks, this should not disrupt the affectionate relationship between the partners.

If it is what the other person *is* rather than what the other person *has* that is the basis for the relationship, then what the person is remains intact. Perhaps this even becomes superior on account of the challenges an individual faces because of the illness.

Marriage, at its root, is the union of two distinct individuals into a soulmate relationship, each one dependent on the other. When the Talmud states that the death of the husband is felt most acutely by the wife and the death of the wife is felt most acutely by the husband (*Sanhedrin* 22b), it speaks directly to this intimate relationship.

It is, therefore, only logical to assume that when one of the marital partners is wrestling with a serious illness, the spouse will feel this with great import. When the relationship is a solid one based on mutual understanding, strong communication, and healthy interaction, then during illness, the partners are able to talk about their feelings.

Partners do wrestle with guilt for not having done enough for the other, and with deep-seated resentment at being abandoned by the other. These are understandable but not necessarily rational emotions. It is best if the partners talk about this openly. This is most likely to happen if the relationship prior to the illness was based on healthy communication. It can hardly be expected that suddenly, because of illness, there will be a dramatic change in the quality of the relationship, although it is not impossible. An improved relationship is a goal that the partners should strive for if they have not been able to attain an ideal level of relationship in healthy times.

I remember speaking to a couple with strong grievances centered around self-centeredness and neglect. I recommended their keeping a daily log of four items: instances when they helped the spouse, instances when they neglected the spouse, instances when the spouse helped them, and instances when the spouse neglected them. After a week, they came back with their lists, and each read the other's list for the first time. Two things happened: Each realized where they had fallen down, and each realized that the other one was not so bad after all. Their shaky marriage took a turn for the better. One of the partners died a short time later, but the surviving partner was left with pleasant memories, rather than negative feelings and guilt over those feelings.

A partner who has been less than fully cooperative in the relationship can, and should, use the situation as it unfolds as an opportunity to make amends. If, for whatever reason—be it because of business pressures or other demands—the spouse was not always at home, now, when illness hits, the opportunity should be used to transcend the previous pattern and to do whatever is possible for one's mate.

Engaging in self-examination and admitting that one was deficient in one's marital responsibilities can help erase the past and dissolve the recriminations that undoubtedly derive from such

deficiency. In other words, illness can be an opportunity not only for the person who is ill, but
for the person or persons most affected by the illness. Whatever improvements are made as a result of this opportunity should be steadfastly kept,
whatever eventually unfolds.

Ice-breaking is vital in dealing with illness.
Some ailing people are reluctant to admit to their
pain or to ask for help. Then there develops a guessing game, with the loved ones often guessing
wrongly, or failing to guess at all.

Bring on the ice-breaker. How difficult is it for
a spouse or a child to beg their loved one, "Please
tell me when you are feeling pain and how the
illness is affecting you, so that I can appreciate this
and react accordingly." This request, though difficult to verbalize, can sometimes work wonders in
terms of alleviating pressures and opening up lines
of communication, which is crucial for recovery.

A person wrestling with illness will become
prey not only to physical fatigue, but also to emotional fatigue. The ailing marital partner, therefore, may not be in the mood for the types of
activity that had characterized the relationship previously. This should not be misinterpreted to mean
that the sick person does not care about or love
the partner in the same way as before. These imag-
inings can make the illness even worse. Lack of
understanding and jumping to wrong conclusions
can add tension and ill-feeling when the ill person and loved ones can least afford it.

Recognizing that direct verbal communication
between loved ones—be they husband–wife or

parent–child—at the time of life-threatening illness is often fraught with difficulty, the couple may want to resort to some form of written communication to lessen the pain that may be involved in direct verbal communication. This is not necessarily a negative commentary on the relationship; often, it is precisely because the relationship is so intense that verbal communication is complicated. The ill person may want to convey how he or she would like to be treated during the illness. Some people want to be pampered; others want to be treated normally. Putting it in writing for the other as a tangible, respectfully expressed request can be very helpful.

Saying "Thank you" to one's partner or child goes a long way toward avoiding the burnout that comes from continual caregiving. Appreciation genuinely expressed energizes those aiding the ailing person to continue what is often a physically enervating and emotionally depleting task.

The expressed feelings of attachment, of love and of warmth, that may be conveyed in writing by a parent to a child are also of great value. Imagine what it means to a child to possess a note in which a parent expresses feelings of love and affection for the child.

Many parents, when preparing their wills, focus much attention on how they want the physical property to be divided after their demise; which one of the children will get this, which one of the children will get that, and so on. But there is nothing wrong—and there is much right—with parents including in their wills testaments to the love they have for their children. This form of expression, in a most tangible document, is further reinforcement of a feeling that is so important for the surviving family.

The same is true for spouses. Thinking beyond one's lifetime precisely at the time that mortality makes a dent in the psyche makes good sense. Taking the time to express one's loving and appreciative feelings is a most precious and everlasting gift, lasting until the ultimate reunion in the ultimate reality of *olam haba*, the World-to-Come.

Concluding Thoughts

This has been a difficult book to write. During its writing, I underwent a whole variety of experiences. Perhaps because I was in the midst of the book, I looked at these experiences differently.

My general distaste for meaningless parties became more marked. My natural tendency to be bothered by small things improved somewhat; now small things bother me less. My tolerance of spiritual occasions reduced to vacuous events nearly disappeared. My appreciation of caring and giving people grew. My admiration for those who nobly endured suffering increased. And my perspective on life changed dramatically.

I sincerely hope that you, the reader, have likewise been affected by this book, and for the better. My guess is that at some junctures in the book, you, the reader, became angry or uneasy. I trust that all this has worked its way out of your system.

In expounding on the Jewish approach to illness and suffering, my goal has been to help ease existing pain by presenting the possible reasons for it, and to help you confront any future illness and suffering by being theologically and psychologically prepared. This book is akin to bitter medicine; it is tough to swallow, but, once swallowed, is more effective than a weak concoction.

Reasons, even hard-to-digest reasons, dull the pain. Preparation hones the readiness to take on the challenge when it comes. We do not, and probably never will, know the reasons for the illness or the suffering, but we are convinced that there is a reason. And the reason is positive and beneficial, not punitive and harmful.

Instead of discovering the reason, we uncover the reason through our self-betterment. We give the illness and suffering a meaning and a purpose consistent with our faith and conviction that the suffering has a purpose.

Judaism's bottom line on illness and suffering is empowerment. This empowerment emanates from the notion that the suffering is in some way related to who we are and what we ought to be. We are therefore empowered with the ability to embrace the proper attitude to our plight. We are empowered to give lasting meaning to illness and suffering by resolving to grow rather than to shrink. We are empowered to help ourselves in both a preventive and a reactive manner.

This is a power that we have not because it is psychologically helpful—which it is—but because God has given us this power and wants us to use it, humbly but effectively. Nothing more need be said.

Hebrew-Language Bibliography

Arukh HaShulhan (8 vols.), Rabbi Yehiel Mikhel Epstein.

Avot D'Rabbe Natan.

Derashot HaRaN.

Derekh Hayyim, Maharal.

Gesher HaHayyim (vol. 1), Rabbi Yehiel Mikhel Tukacinsky, Jerusalem (private printing), 1960.

Hatam Sofer Responsa, Rabbi Mosheh Sofer.

Hovot Halevovot, Rabbi Bahya ben Yosef ibn Pekuda.

Iggeret HaKodesh (The Holy Letter), attributed to Rabbi Moses Nahmanides.

Igrot Mosheh (Hoshen Mishpat 2), Rabbi Mosheh Feinstein, Bnai Brak: Ohel Yosef Printers, 1985.

Kad HaKemah, Rabbi Bahya ben Yosef ibn Pekuda.

Kol Bo al Avelut, Rabbi Yekutiel Yehudah Greenwald, New York: Feldheim, 1965.

Maharal, commentary on Talmud.

Mekhilta.

Midrash Rabbah.
Midrash Tanhuma.
Mikraot Gedolot al HaTorah.
Mishnah Berurah, Rabbi Yisrael Meir HaKohen.
Mishnah Torah, Rabbi Moses Maimonides.
Netiv HaYisurin, in *Netivot Olam*, Maharal.
Pele Yoetz, Rabbi Eliezer Papo.
Perush HaMishnayot (commentary to the Mishnah), Rabbi Moses Maimonides.
Pesikta.
Sefer Ben Sira (Ecclesiasticus).
Sefer Hahinukh, Aaron of Barcelona.
Sefer HaKuzari, Rabbi Yehudah HaLevi.
Sefer Haredim, Rabbi Elazar Azikri.
Sefer Hasidim, Rabbi Yehudah HaHasid.
Shelah—Asarah Ma'amarot.
Shever Gaon, in *Hibur HaTeshuvah L'Rabbenu Menahem ben R' Shelomoh HaMeiri.*
Shulhan Arukh, Rabbi Yosef Karo.
Sifri.
Talmud Bavli (Babylonian Talmud).
Talmud Yerushalmi (Jerusalem Talmud).
Tanya, Rabbi Shneur Zalman of Liadi.
Tiferet Yisrael on Mishnayot.
Torah Temimah (5 vols.), Rabbi Barukh HaLevi Epstein.
Tosefta.
Yalkut Shimoni.
Ziz Eliezer (17 vols.), Rabbi Eliezer Waldenburg.
Zohar al Hamishah Humshay Torah.

English-Language Bibliography

Berkovits, Eliezer. *Faith After the Holocaust*. New York: Ktav Publishing House, 1973.

Boteach, Shmuel. *Wrestling with the Divine: A Jewish Response to Suffering*. Northvale, New Jersey: Jason Aronson, 1995.

Bulka, Reuven P. *The Quest for Ultimate Meaning: Principles and Applications of Logotherapy*. New York: Philosophical Library, 1979.

Bulka, Reuven P. *Jewish Marriage: An Halakhic Ethic*. New York and Hoboken: Ktav Publishing House and Yeshiva University Press, 1986.

Bulka, Reuven P. *Chapters of the Sages: A Psychological Commentary on Pirkey Avoth*. Northvale, New Jersey: Jason Aronson, 1993.

Bulka, Reuven P. *Judaism on Pleasure*. Northvale, New Jersey: Jason Aronson, 1995.

Frankl, Viktor. "The Philosophical Foundations of Logotherapy," in Erwin W. Straus (ed.), *Phenom-*

enology: Pure and Applied. Pittsburgh: Duquesne University Press, 1964, pp. 43–59.

Frankl, Viktor. *The Doctor and the Soul: From Psychotherapy to Logotherapy*. New York: Bantam Books, 1967.

Frankl, Viktor. *Man's Search for Meaning: An Introduction to Logotherapy*. New York: Washington Square Press, 1968.

Frankl, Viktor. *The Will to Meaning: Foundations and Applications of Logotherapy*. New York: The New American Library, 1969.

Hirsch, Rabbi Samson Raphael. *The Pentateuch: Translated & Explained* (6 vols.) (trans. by Isaac Levy). London: 1963.

The Holy Scriptures (3 vols.). Philadelphia: Jewish Publication Society, 1982.

Lamm, Maurice. *The Power of Hope*. New York: Simon & Schuster, 1995.

Maimonides, Moses. *The Guide of the Perplexed* (trans. by Shlomo Pines). Chicago: University of Chicago Press, 1963.

Midrash (10 vols.), H. Freedman and M. Simon (eds.). London: Soncino Press, 1961.

Nahmanides, Moses. *Writings & Discourses*, vol. 2 (trans. and annotated by C. B. Chavel). New York: Shilo Publishing House, 1978.

"Of God and Weinerville." *The New York Times Magazine*, December 10, 1995, 58; 60–61.

"Paralyzed judge 'living as best I can with ALS.'" *Canadian Jewish News*, December 7, 1995, 21.

Saadia Gaon. *The Book of Beliefs and Opinions* (trans. by Samuel Rosenblatt). New Haven: Yale University Press, 1948.

Talmud (18 vols.). I. Epstein (ed.). London: Soncino Press, 1961.

Tanna debe Eliyahu: The Lore of the School of Elijah. (trans. by W. Braude & I. Kapstein). Philadelphia: Jewish Publication Society, 1981.

Wurzburger, Walter. *Ethics of Responsibility: Pluralistic Approaches to Covenantal Ethics*. Philadelphia: Jewish Publication Society, 1994.

Index

ABOUT THE AUTHOR

Reuven P. Bulka received ordination from Rabbi Jacob Joseph Rabbinical Seminary in 1965 and a Ph.D. in Logotherapy from the University of Ottawa in 1971. He has been Rabbi of Congregation Machzikei Hadas in Ottawa since 1967 and founding editor of the *Journal of Psychology and Judaism* since 1976. Host of the weekly TV series "In Our Hands" and the radio call-in program "Religion on the Air," he is also chaplain of the Dominion Command of the Royal Canadian Legion, President of the International Rabbinic Forum of Keren HaYesod, chairman of the Rabbinic Cabinet for State of Israel Bonds in Canada, chairman of the Religious and Inter-Religious Affairs Committee of Canadian Jewish Congress, and Chairman of the Religious Advisory Committee for United Way of Ottawa-Carlton. He is author or editor of thirty books and 100 articles on psychology- and Judaism-related themes, and his books are syndicated in various national newspapers.